Dumbocracy

Why American elections so often go horribly wrong

Robert B. Chamberlain, PhD, ThD

"Everything is changing. People are taking their comedians seriously and the politicians as a joke."
— Will Rogers [1895-1972]

<u>Notice</u>

Dumbocracy
Why American elections so often go horribly wrong

Copyright © 2015
Robert B. Chamberlain, PhD, ThD

All rights reserved. No portion of this book may be reproduced or transmitted in any form or by any means, digital, electronic or mechanical, including transcription, recording, photocopying, digitization, or by any information storage and retrieval system, without permission in writing from the author.

Independently Published 2015
Charleston, South Carolina, USA
ISBN: 978-1514349731

The author

 The author of this book (and those listed on the next page) is Dr. Robert B. Chamberlain, PhD, ThD. His professional life featured a successful management career at one of the largest private corporations in the world; but, following an early retirement, Dr. Chamberlain initiated a "second career" teaching Cultural Anthropology and World Religions at Eastern Florida State College. Although having authored several earlier texts, all of his published works have been written during his time at the college.

Dr. Chamberlain has what might be called an eclectic education: holding a BSEE (Bachelor of Science) in Electrical Engineering; MSEE (Master of Science) in Electrical Engineering, specializing in Computer Science; post-graduate work in Ergonomics (Human Factors Engineering); a PhD (Doctor of Philosophy) in Cultural Anthropology, with documented sub-specializations in Cross-Cultural Management, and Comparative Religions; and, a ThD (Doctor of Theology) specializing in Christian Apologetics.

He and his wife, Pamela, have two adult children and four grandchildren, and currently live on the east coast of Florida with their dog, Alex (a Sheltie), and several cats.

Books in Print

- **An Introduction to World Religions**   ISBN: 978-1484891605
  A general introduction to the major religions of the world developed
  as a college textbook for a course at Eastern Florida State College.

- **An Introduction to Cultural Anthropology**   ISBN: 978-1490392301
  A general introduction to Cultural Anthropology developed as a college textbook for a course at Eastern Florida State College.

- **In the Shadows:** *Conspiracy*   ISBN: 978-1500561031
  Every murder or assassination spawns conspiracy theories; but, a review of the facts says most of them may be true.

- **Dumbocracy**   ISBN: 978-1514349731
  Why American elections so often go horribly wrong (with examples).

Tetralogy: *Christ – from a pragmatic viewpoint*
A critical look at Jesus (Christ) that recognizes the miraculous nature
of his life while also offering possible non-miraculous explanations.

- **Book 1: The Life of Christ**   ISBN: 978-1477552322
  Christ's physical life: from virgin birth to crucifixion.

- **Book 2: The Miracles of Christ**   ISBN: 978-1478263654
  A review of over two dozen "miracles" attributed to Christ.

- **Book 3: The Resurrection of Christ**   ISBN: 978-1479317806
  Accounts from Persia and India that tell of the years after the
  crucifixion — recounting a possible life in northern India.

- **Book 4: The Teachings of Christ**   ISBN: 978-1508518938
  In addition to what Christ instructed his followers to do, what is
  in his words and actions that addresses modern ethical issues?

Earlier texts were written as gifts for a church, an historical
society, or as "works for hire" while an employee of GE. These
texts are no longer in print, and are no longer available.

- A History of Rowley, Massachusetts [editor]
- The First Church of Christ, Scientist – Marblehead
- The Jewel Mill: A 17th Century Millsite
- The Published Works of L. Ivimy Gwalter [editor]
- A Beginner's Introduction to Computer Programming in BASIC
- Practical Statistics for Engineers
- A 4-part Guide for US – India Globalization
- A Guide for US – México Globalization (English & Spanish editions)

Dumbocracy
Why American elections so often go horribly wrong

Table of Contents

Foreword

No one in this world, so far as I know—and I have searched the records for years, and employed agents to help me—has ever lost money by underestimating the intelligence of the great masses of the plain people. — HL Mencken

"Civilization, in fact, grows more and more maudlin and hysterical; especially under democracy it tends to degenerate into a mere combat of crazes; the whole aim of practical politics is to keep the populace alarmed (and hence clamorous to be led to safety) by menacing it with an endless series of hobgoblins, most of them imaginary." This quote, from HL Mencken's *In Defense of Women* (1918) illustrates the basic premise of this book. The republican form of government, where the electorate selects representatives to govern in their interest has, throughout human history, shown a consistent tendency to beome "more and more maudlin and hysterical". The representatives that are elected frequently appear to be the least logical of the choices; nevertheless, they not only get elected, they often get <u>re</u>-elected!

Politicians who have been convicted of theft, embezzlement, and misuse of public funds get re-elected to the same positions from which they stole, embezzled, or abused the public trust. Others have clearly demonstrated either a lack of morals or intelligence, and yet are repeatedly sent back to office to legislate new laws. Any rational, reasonable citizen asks why the public does this. And, that is a valid question.

Here, we will explore several possible reasons why these seemingly incomprehensible electoral results occur. It is rarely just one reason, though; most cases are a combination of several reasons. However, there usually does appear to be one particular aspect of the candidate or election that was the primary driver behind these irrational results. Following a brief overview of how the American government was designed and intended to work, we'll take a look at what so often happens anyway. This can be described as a *good plan,* but *flawed execution.*

Section I
The Process As It Was Designed

The American governmental structure was designed by some of the brightest people of the 18th century. After the American Revolution was won, these men followed the intent and goals outlined in the *Declaration of Independence*. They created a loose confederation (with a weak central government) out of the thirteen newly independent states (former British colonies), and wrote the *Articles of Confederation* to govern it.

When flaws in this confederation became apparent in the years that followed, they took a bold step: rather than modify, adjust, or "tweak" the *Articles*, they completely rethought the structural formation of the central government. The result of this approach is what is known today as the *Constitution of the United States*.

This *Constitution* specifies what powers and authority is vested in the central government, and which were retained by the state (formerly colonial) governments. These individual state governments each developed an individual constitution unique to them, and further broke down the operation of government into smaller entities (such as counties, parishes, cities, towns, villages, *et cetera*).

Nearly all of these various governmental levels were set up to operate as *republics*; but, there were a few exceptions that were true democracies (*eg* New England town meeting governments). Therefore, the problems that arise when the "wrong people" are elected to office occur exclusively within republican entities (as true democracies typically don't elect anyone to represent them).

Many other nations have similar governmental features, where members of Parliament and a chief executive officer (typically, a Prime Minister) are chosen (*e.g.* Great Britain, Germany, Italy, France, India, Japan, Australia, New Zealand, Brazil, *et cetera*). And, although the examples used here to illustrate where things so often go wrong are all drawn from the United States, similar idiocy has occurred in virtually every elected government.

Chapter 1
The American Government

The government, which was designed for the people, has got into the hands of the bosses and their employers, the special interests. An invisible empire has been set up above the forms of democracy.   — Woodrow Wilson

The central (*i.e.* federal) government of the United States was established under the *Constitution* to operate in three distinct branches: executive, legislative, and judicial. The stated intent was that each of these branches would have not only their own specific functions and roles, but would also serve to keep the other two from exceeding their assigned areas of operation — a so-called system of "checks and balances".

Executive

[The American President] has to take all sorts of abuse from liars and demagogues.... The people can never understand why the President does not use his supposedly great power to make 'em behave. Well, all the President is, is a glorified public relations man who spends his time flattering, kissing and kicking people to get them to do what they are supposed to do anyway.   — President Harry S. Truman

The Executive Branch of the US government consists of the President, Vice-President, and a number of other officials. It has primary responsibility for the approval, implementation, and enforcement of the laws enacted by the Legislative Branch, and the application of the interpretation of those laws (as well as of the Constitution) deemed valid by the Judicial Branch.

The President, as head of the Executive Branch, approves and implements government policy and laws. S/he is elected to a four year term, and is limited to no more than 2½ terms (beginning with an Amendment to the Consitution passed after Franklin Roosevelt had been elected to 4 consecutive terms). The President does have the power to veto laws passed by the Legislative Branch, but the veto fails if ⅔ of the 2 houses of the Legislature repass it.

The President negotiates treaties (which must then be approved by the Senate), acts as the Head of State, serves as Commander-in-Chief of the military, and nominates those who serve in the Judiciary or as head of one of the Cabinet Level Departments,

Cabinet Level Departments have been added, changed and removed over the history of the country. The head of each department is referred to as the "Secretary of …"; and, their function is to provide advice to the President and oversight of their deparments. As of 2015, there are 15 such departments:
- State
- Treasury
- Defense
- Justice
- Interior
- Agriculture
- Commerce
- Labor
- Health and Human Services
- Homeland Security
- Housing and Urban Development
- Transportation
- Education
- Energy
- Veterans' Affairs

Currently, the President and Vice-President are elected as a team (it was not always that way), and are selected in an indirect electoral process. All eligible voters (essentially, all citizens aged 18 or older) vote for the team of their choice. Each team has a list of *electors* selected by state, and equal in number to the sum total of Congressmen and Senators that represent that state. Those electors that were selected by the team that wins a plurality of the votes cast then get to cast votes that are counted by Congress. These electors were chosen by the various teams, and pledged to vote for that particular team. On rare occasions, some electors have violated that pledge, as there is no legal requirement for them to honor it. Typically the team that wins a plurality of the votes gets all of the *electoral votes* from that state (*i.e.* the number of representatives the state has in the Legislative Branch: 2 Senators + the proportional number of Representatives).

This system was set up to provide each state both a population-based proportion of influence (for the number of Reps assigned to that state) in addition to an "every state equal" proportion (for the 2 Senators each has). Although this system has been in effect for centuries, it has only rarely become an issue — typically when the President/Vice-President team elected is not the team that received the most votes of the citizens nationwide. This has happened just four times in US history (1824, 1876, 1888, and 2000). There are also special rules if none of the President/Vice-President teams wins a majority of these *Electoral Votes*. However, this has only happened once (1824).

Legislative

> *The oppressed are allowed once every few years to decide which particular representatives of the oppressing class are to represent and repress them in parliament.*
> — Soviet Leader Vladimir Lenin

> *If 'pro' is the opposite of 'con', what is the opposite of 'progress'?* — Commentator Paul Harvey

The Legislative Branch consists of two "houses" of Congress (called a *bicameral* legislature): the Senate and the House of Representatives. There are two Senators from each state, which gives every state an "equal say" in Senate activities; and, senators are elected for a term of 6 years. Their primary functions are: to vote on new laws; approve (or disapprove) Presidential nominations to the Cabinet, the Supreme Court, federal courts, and other posts; and, to ratify treaties (requiring a two-thirds majority).

The House of Representatives is proportionately based on the state populations. Every state is entitled to have at least one representative, and the total changed frequently as the population of the country grew. Beginning in 1911, the total number of members of the House of Representatives was set at 435. In 2015, each Representative thus represented approximately 735,000 citizens.

Judicial

> *I will be vigilant to protect the independence and integrity of the Supreme Court, and I will work to ensure that it upholds the rule of law and safeguards those liberties that make this land one of endless possibilities for all Americans.*
> — Chief Justice John Roberts

> *Presidents come and go, but the Supreme Court goes on forever.*   —William Howard Taft[1]

The Judicial Branch has oversight of the court system of the country. It consists of three levels of federal courts:

- 94 District Courts, which are distributed around the country (at least one in each state, the District of Columbia, and Puerto Rico) and in three US Territories (Guam, US Virgin Islands, and Northern Mariana Islands).

- 12 Appellate Courts, which each have authority to hear appeals from a specified circuit of the District Courts.

- The Supreme Court, which has final oversight of the US Court System.

A primary role of the Supreme Court has been to interpret the Constitution and rule on whether or not specific laws are constitutional (*i.e.* comply with the Constitution). It consists of nine justices: a *Chief Justice*, who supervises the court's operation; and, eight *Associate Justices*, All Supreme Court decisions are made by a majority vote of the Court. Justices are nominated by the President, approved by the Senate, and appointed for life (or until their resignation). Their decisions can not be over-ruled by any other court or by the President, and their decisions have often set a precedent for interpreting the laws.

---

1 Taft had a unique perspective on these two roles: in the only instance of its kind, William Howard Taft served first as President (1909-1913), and then later as Chief Justice of the Supreme Court (1921-1930).

Chapter 2
American Goals & Expectations

The worst government is the most moral. One composed of cynics is often very tolerant and humane. But when fanatics are on top there is no limit to oppression.   — HL Mencken

From their first day in school, Americans are educated to believe that their country is a "shining beacon" of liberty and human rights to the rest of the world. They're told that the so-called *American experiment* is an example of what intelligent, well-intentioned people can do when motivated to create, as Lincoln described it, a "government of the people, by the people, for the people". The result of this is that Americans are, by and large, an extremely ethnocentric society. That is not a criticism; it is just an observation from a trained anthropologist.

This ethnocentricity inevitably leads to unrealistic expectations and unattainable goals. The very basis of capitalism is the pursuit of financial gain and commercial expansion; and, the result of this can be seen in the reaction of the stock market when a business reports earnings that are stable and profitable. The typical reaction is one of disappointment. The annual expectation in the financial markets is that retail establishments will show at least several percentage points of growth in sales and profits per outlet per year. The problem is that this is not indefinitely sustainable without a corresponding increase in population. If a population is stable, aggregate sales and profits in the marketplace are capped by the limit of disposable income available to that population.

Goals and expectations are similarly unrealistic when it comes to the political arena. Voters expect that their elected officials will resolve any challenges to the country and the people, and that they will effectively control circumstances such that foreign powers are unable to disrupt or damage the typical American lifestyle.

- Great Britain limited and/or deprived the colonists of control over their own destiny. The result was a revolution that "sent them packing".

- When a suspicious explosion destroyed a US battleship anchored in Havana harbor, the US government responded by going to war, and defeating the Spanish Empire.

    (At 9:40 PM on February 15th, 1898, the *USS Maine*, while at anchor in Havana harbor, exploded — killing 260 men on board. Although the cause of the explosion has <u>never</u> been satisfactorily determined, the US declared war on Spain on April 25th. Over the next 3½ months, the US defeated Spain and was awarded sovereignty over Cuba, Puerto Rico, the Philippines, and Guam.)

- Germany acted belligerently against US interests in the First World War. The US joined with the Allies to ensure their defeat.

    (On May 7th, 1915, a German submarine torpedoed the *RMS Lusitania*, a British passenger ship that had left New York 6 days earlier on its voyage to Liverpool, England. 1,198 of those on board were killed (including 128 Americans). Attacks of this sort continued into early 1916 with Germany engaged in unrestricted submarine warfare in the Atlantic – sinking both merchant and passenger ships. In March, after sinking an unarmed French ship in the English Channel [the *Sussex*], Germany pledged not to attack passenger ships in the future. On January 31st, 1917, however, Germany informed the US of its intention to resume unrestricted submarine warfare; and, in April that same year, the US declared war on Germany and entered World War I on the side of the Allied Powers (Great Britain, Russia, France, and Italy). A year and a half later, the war ended with a resounding Allied victory.)

- Japan bombed the US fleet in Hawai'i on a Sunday. Again, the US went to war to "make them pay"; and, they did.

    (On December 7th, 1941, 353 Japanese aircraft from the Imperial Japanese Navy bombed Pearl Harbor, Honolulu, Hawai'i. 2,403 Americans were killed, and another 1,178 were injured. As a result, the US entered into World War II on the side of the Allies. By the time that the war finally ended with Japanese surrender — August 15th, 1945 — somewhere between 50 and 85 million people had been killed. It was the deadliest conflict in world history.)

- al-Qaeda operatives commandeered 4 commercial planes and deliberately crashed them in 2001. The response was

to go to war in Afghanistan to destroy their base of operation, and wreak havoc on them.

Time after time, when America has been attacked or abused by
a foreign power, it has responded with force and determination;
and, the result has nearly always been a resounding American
victory. Americans have actually come to expect this from their
leaders. Even in those rare defeats, American leaders have had the
audacity to simply declare victory!

In January of 1973, all of the parties involved in the Viet Nam
War (the United States, North Viet Nam, South Viet Nam, and
other US allies) signed an agreement in Paris titled *Agreement on
Ending the War and Restoring Peace in Viet Nam*. President Nixon then effectively 'declared victory'. Victory? We had more than
half a million troops in a country roughly the size of Florida, had
seen 282,000 allied troops killed in action (nearly 46,000 of whom
were American), and basically got our asses kicked! But, the
American people expect the US to come out of whatever we do
with victory. Nixon couldn't disappoint them, so he declared
victory.

Americans have come to expect a successful conclusion of any
task to which their leaders put their minds: military, economic,
diplomatic, *et cetera*. The fact that this has often been the case has
only served to reinforce that expectation.

The *Great Depression* devastated the economies of countries
all over the world. The US was no exception. But, the capitalist
system of the United States, resting firmly on the intelligence and
resilience of the American people, would resolve the problems.
Right? That's certainly what Americans thought; and, in hind-
sight, that is precisely what most Americans think happened. But,
was that really what ended the Depression?

Despite heroic efforts on the part of President Franklin Delano
Roosevelt, the US economy was still struggling a full decade after
the 1929 Stock Market crash. Capitalism works, but it was
severely tested by the Depression. So, what ended the *Great
Depression*? There were a lot of factors; but, without doubt, the
greatest impact on the economy was the US entering into World

War II with a full war-time economy[2]. Everybody went to work to support the war effort.

American ethnocentricity and high expectations are well documented, and the typical American voter would never support a candidate who suggested anything that ran counter to them. For that reason, American political candidates repeatedly promise full employment, low taxes, more opportunity, and "peace in our time".[3] Repeatedly, leaders have either explicitly or implicitly promised these objectives. Unfortunately, these promises have often gone unfulfilled.

---

2 In the 85 years following the 1929 crash, the three highest GDP (Gross Domestic Product) increases occurred in 1941, 1942, and 1943 (17.7%, 18.9%, and 17.0%, respectively).

3 This phrase was made famous when British Prime Minister Neville Chamberlain stood outside his official residence at 10 Downing Street, and announced on September 30, 1938 that the *Munich Agreement* with Hitler had secured "peace for our time". Less than a year later, Europe was totally embroiled in World War II.

Chapter 3

The Electoral Process

*Elections belong to the people. It's their decision. If they de-
cide to turn their back on the fire and burn their behinds, then
they will just have to sit on their blisters* — Abraham Lincoln.

*Half of the American people have never read a newspaper.
Half never voted for President. One hopes it is the same half.*
　　　　　　　　　　　　　　　　　　　　 — Gore Vidal

So, how does the American electoral process work? It depends
on the level about which you are talking. At the local level,
individuals choose to run for office, campaign for election, and the
candidate that receives the highest number of votes is declared the
winner and assumes the office. Some jurisdictions require a clear
majority; and, if nobody gets one, then the top two candidates have
a "runoff" election to determine the winner.

At the state level, the states typically have a system that mimics
the local systems in most of their parts. Candidates decide to run
for a particular office, and then campaign for that office. If they
get the most votes from the electorate, they are declared the victor,
and assume that office on the specified date.

Nationally, it gets a little more complicated. Some offices
work much the same way as the local and state offices do; but, the
highest offices (*i.e.* President and Vice-President) are actually an
indirect electoral process. Voters often believe they are voting for
these candidates, but are actually voting for a slate of people chos-
en by the candidates' people to become *electors*. These electors
have promised, or pledged, to cast their vote for the candidate that
chose them; but, they are not legally required to do so.

When a particular candidate's "ticket" receives the most votes,
their slate of electors is declared victorious and those electors then
cast their votes for President and Vice-President. These votes are
delivered in sealed envelopes to Congress, where they are opened
and counted in the House of Representatives. The Presidential
ticket that is found to have a majority of these *electoral votes* is

then declared the winner. Although the outcome is usually a fore-gone conclusion, there have occasionally been surprises when an elector chose to cast their vote for someone other than the candi-date who had placed them on that slate.[4]

What is missing in these descriptions is the concept of *political parties*. These are essentially 'private clubs', and were not actually set up by the Constitution. Very early in American history, it was common to have several people contending for the same office. For example, George Washington decided in 1796 that he would not run again. In that election, several people ran to replace him:

- John Adams (Vice-President)
- Thomas Jefferson (former Secretary of State)
- Aaron Burr (US Senator from New York)
- Samuel Adams (Massachusetts Governor)
- Oliver Ellsworth (Supreme Court Chief Justice)
- Thomas Pinckney (former South Carolina Governor)
- John Jay (New York Governor)

This election was very close, and the results were not what any of the candidates had wanted: Vice-President John Adams won the presidency; but, his chief opponent, Thomas Jefferson, was elected Vice-President. One consequence of this was the 12th Amendment to the Constitution (ratified in 1804) which, since that point, has the President and Vice President run as a team. Another result was the increasing importance of political parties. Like minded people determined that if they could agree on their candidates prior to an election, everyone who favored that view would be voting for the same candidate – giving them a much better chance of winning.

Since the US does not have a parliamentary form of government (which often relies on a coalition of parties to form a legislative majority), common sense dictates that a two-party

---

4 For example in 1960, 15 electors (8-Mississippi, 6-Alabama, 1-Oklahoma) refused to honor their pledges, and cast their votes for Virginia Senator Harry F. Byrd instead of Kennedy. Their decision, however, was not significant enough to alter the outcome of the election. In 1980, a Republican elector from Washington pledged to President Gerald Ford cast their vote for Cali-fornia Governor Ronald Reagan. But, President Ford would have lost even with that vote.

system is the most competitive. As a result, smaller parties (usually known collectively as *third parties*) are usually irrelevant to the outcome of an election — usually, but not always.

Only on rare occasions has a new, minor, or third party grown to become a prime contender in a national election. The Whig Party effectively disintegrated in the 1850s, and former Whigs migrated to other parties: conservative Whigs usually migrated to the American Party (often called the *Know Nothing Party*), while northern, liberal Whigs mostly shifted to the new Republican Party. The American Party only lasted a few years, but the Republican Party became a permanent fixture on the political scene, and elected its first presidential ticket in 1860 (Abraham Lincoln and Hannibal Hamlin).

Political parties are essentially private, membership organizations. As such, the government really has no involvement in the operation of these parties; but, when the entire membership of the party is involved, and the outcome of that participation has such a strong impact on the electoral process, the government has a responsibility to ensure that the process is fair and legal. This is the reason that there is government oversight of primary elections – those elections which help to decide the party's candidate in an election.

Section II

Why We Fail: Flawed Execution

*The best argument against democracy is a five-minute conver-
sation with the average voter.*
— UK Prime Minister Winston S Churchill

As was stated at the beginning of Section I, "the American governmental structure was designed by some of the brightest people of the 18th century." And, when you consider those factors which the typical election involves, it would be reasonable to expect that some very good people would be elected to office. What are these factors?

- a rigorous, well designed electoral process;

- more than two centuries of election experience that produces a smooth and peaceful transfer of power;

- one of the best educated electorates in the world;

- an extended campaign period during which candidates have virtually unrestricted opportunity to "make their case" to the voters; and,

- an independent, aggressive media dedicated to uncovering anything they believe the populace ought to, or would want to, know.

So why, then, do American elections so often go horribly wrong? To answer this, we must first agree on what we mean here by "horribly wrong". An ultra-conservative voter from rural Alabama might consider the election of an ultra-liberal candidate from Connecticut to be a disaster; but, what if that is what the majority of the electorate chose? Although it might be seen as a disaster by that southern voter, it would not have gone "horribly wrong". The system would have worked the way it was supposed to work, the way it was designed to work.

Consider, however, the case where an elected official is arrested, charged, indicted, tried, and convicted of embezzling thousands of dollars of tax money and using it to support his mistress. That would be a terrible breach of both his marriage vows and the public trust. If, however, that official ran for re-election to the same position from which he had stolen the money *and won*, that would be an electoral process that had gone horribly wrong. The system was never designed to put people in positions of power if history had already shown that they were neither morally, ethically, nor legally equipped to handle it.

So, what could lead to such a misguided electoral process? Despite the competent design of the American system, it fails with flawed execution. What factors could lead to such a flawed execution?

- Memory Loss – the voter typically has many things on their mind, and may not recall earlier indiscretions by the candidate. This memory loss may be from "brain overload", or it could be a deliberate, subconscious memory failure to provide self-justification for their vote.

- Attention Deficit – similar to memory loss, except that the voter never really developed an understanding of what it was that the candidate had done because their attention was drawn to something else. The event in question may not have been public knowledge when they voted; or, it might have been public knowledge, but not in a form readily understood by the voter.

- Ignorance – as the fictional character Forrest Gump once said, "Stupid is as stupid does." There is no intelligence test that is a prerequisite to vote. This does not mean that the voters lack fundamental intelligence, but only that there may be areas where they are intensely ignorant.

- Greed – the voters may overlook a lot in their candidate if there is 'something in it for them'. This is not the greed of the candidate, but the more subtle greed of the electorate.

- Hero Worship – the candidate is a "hero" in their eyes, and can therefore "do no wrong". They "won the war", "saved the republic", "rallied the economy", or some other noteworthy act that earned the voters' trust and admiration.

- Tunnel Vision – nothing matters to the electorate except for some single issue; and, on that issue, the candidate is saying and doing what the electorate wants. All of the other candidate's positions on other issues are thus cosidered inconsequential.

- Manipulation – external forces have used power, position, or money to manipulate the system such that the typical voter never learns of an impropriety, or is given such a slanted view of it that they feel justified in ignoring it (perhaps even admiring it).

- Fear – actually, *reactive fear*; there are very few emotions more potent than fear. When one candidate for office finds a way to get us to truly fear what would happen if their opponent were to win, we can overlook almost anything about that candidate. The logic goes something like "I can live with anything so long as *Candidate X* doesn't get the chance to destroy me, my income, our society, and everything that I hold dear".

In this section, we'll consider each of these factors, and look at examples where they have apparently been a major contributing factor. Then, in the next Section, we'll examine the consequences of these decisions.

Chapter 4
Memory Loss

Time and memory are true artists; they remould reality nearer to the heart's desire.   — John Dewey

Without memory, there is no culture. Without memory, there would be no civilization, no society, no future. — Elie Weisel

John Dewey (author of the 1st epigraph above) was a philosopher, psychologist and reformer who was well known as a staunch defender of democracy (in all fields, not just government). The quote above is insightful in that Dewey sees memory as not just a mental filing system, but primarily as a creative function — one that "remould[s] reality".

Elie Weisel, recipient of numerous awards for his political activism in pursuit of justice for the victims of the Nazi death camps[5], adds to Dewey's statement by saying that "without memory, there would be no civilization, no society, no future." And yet, voters all over the world consciously or unconsciously suppress memories as they choose their leaders, their representatives, and their policies.

"He did what? I don't remember that!" That might very well be the answer one would get when questioning a voter about the vote they just cast for a particular candidate. If there had been some established, proven, unquestioned malfeasance on the part of the candidate; and, if they voted for them anyway, it might be easier to say that their mind was "someplace else", that they "forgot", when they cast their vote than to admit their error.

There may have been one of any number of reasons why their memory appears to have failed them once they entered the polling booth; and, we'll explore some of these in the chapters that follow.

---

5 Weisel has been awarded the Nobel Peace Prize, Presidential Medal of Freedom (US), Congressional Gold Medal (US), Order of the Star of Romania, Legion of Honor (France), Order of the British Empire (UK), and numerous other tributes.

But, the bottom line remains the same regardless of the reasons: they simply did not "remember" how bad the candidate was when they cast their vote. They had "forgotten" the actions or statements that make support for their candidate illogical, if not criminal.

Someone defending the voter's actions might ask if what the candidate had done was really all that bad. Well,

- what if they had been videotaped using an illegal drug (*e.g.* cocaine), arrested, tried, convicted, and even sentenced to jail time?

- what if they had been stopped driving their car in the middle of the night without lights, legally drunk, and in the company of a stripper with whom they had had a fight, continued their relationship with the stripper, admitted to being an alcoholic, held a press conference (while drunk) in the stripper's dressing room at a burlesque theater where she was performing — all while holding the most sensitive and powerful position in Congress?

- what if they had been arrested, tried, convicted, and served time in prison after being charged with conspiracy, extortion, racketeering, mail fraud, and witness tampering? what if a close aide was even videotaped accepting a bribe on behalf of the candidate?

- what if they had been convicted on multiple occasions, had spent time in federal prison, had frequently used their connections with organized crime to accomplish their ends, and called one of their opponents a communist while playing to the ethnic bigotry in parts of their constituency?

Example #1:

Washington, D.C. Mayor Marion Barry

Marion Shepilov Barry, Jr. [1936 – 2014] was only the second elected mayor of Washington, DC, and was elected to 4 terms (serving from 1979 to 1991, and then from 1995 to 1999) — nobody else has ever been elected to more than 2 terms — and, in every oath of office Mayor Barry took, it began with "I, Marion Barry, do solemnly swear that I will faithfully execute the laws of the United States of America and of the District of Columbia". When not mayor, Barry was elected to the DC Council (the District legislature) 5 times, and served in that capacity for 16 years (having held the office for 10 conecutive years at the time of his death in November, 2014).

Barry was arrested after smoking crack on videotape prior to having sex with an ex-girlfriend in a local hotel room. He was charged with 3 felony counts of perjury, and 10 counts of possession of a controlled substance. Although the jury hung on most of the charges, he was convicted on one count of possession, and served 6 months in federal prison. Media investigations after the trial revealed that 5 of the jurors were convinced that the prosecution had falsified evidence in a racist conspiracy, while the other 7 considered the evidence both legitimate and overwhelmingly convincing of his guilt. They even rejected evidence that the defense had never contested! The judge scolded the jurors for not following instructions, but was forced to declare a mistrial on those charges.

After his release, he was elected to the City Council until he was re-elected mayor 2 years later. The electorate obviously either didn't care, or had a very short memory. The alternative Washington newspaper *Washington City Paper* nicknamed him "Mayor for Life". Evidently, a large portion of the electorate agreed with them. Barry was extremely popular with the poorest members of the city, and this undoubtedly led to their very short memories. Periodically, Barry made public statements that can only be described as outlandish:

- "What right does Congress have to go around making laws just because they deem it necessary?"

- "Outside of the killings, Washington has one of the lowest crime rates in the country."

Videotaped smoking crack cocaine prior to cheating on his wife by engaging in sex with an ex-girlfriend; arrested by the FBI; indicted on multiple counts of perjury and drug possession; tried in court, and found guilty of possession; sentenced to jail time, and served 6 months in federal prison — and they *re-elected* him?

It would appear that the voters of Washington, DC were highly, conveniently forgetful when it came to the "indiscretions" of their mayor. They may have had their reasons (some of these will be explored in future chapters), but regardless of their reasons, they were more than willing to "forget" the problems.

Drug use, however, is far from the only issue that the electorate seems to be able to easily forget. They also seem to be able to forget elected officials' drunken escapades and illicit sexual relationships with strippers.

Technically, getting drunk – even being an alcolholic – is not illegal; and, neither is having sex with a married stripper. The media seems convinced that the public has a right to know about the morals of their elected officials, however; and, this next example of electoral forgetfulness certainly questions their morality.

OK. Wilbur Mills fell victim to temptations; and, so have many other politicians, entertainers and sports stars. But, how does that account for the apparent memory lapse of the electorate just a month later? How do they account for the apparent idiocy of re-electing someone so clearly vulnerable to such a sensitive position, one of such immense power?

Example #2:

US Representative Wilbur Mills

Wilbur Daigh Mills (1909 – 1992) was elected to Congress from the 2nd District of Arkansas 19 consecutive times (38 years). The final 17 years of that time was spent as Chairman of the House Ways and Means Committee. He was so powerful in Congress that he was even briefly a candidate for the 1972 Democratic nomination for President.

Ways and Means has been described as the most powerful committee in Congress – members are not even allowed to serve on another committee. They have oversight of Social Security, Medicare, Unemployment, Temporary Assistance for Needy Families, Adoption, Foster care, Child Support, and all tax, tariff, and revenue actions. This makes the Chairmanship of that Committee a _very_ sensitive position.

On October 9, 1974 (at 2:00 AM), Mills was stopped in Washington DC (by US Park Police) for driving erratically without his headlights on: drunk, his face cut and bruised from a fight with his stipper-mistress, Fannie Foxe (_aka_ Annabelle Battistella). Foxe, from Argentina, jumped from the car and into the DC Tidal Basin, trying to escape without being caught with Mills. She was taken into custody.

Despite the impropriety of the situation, Mills was re-elected (for the 18th time) with nearly 60% of the vote just a month later. Just 25 days after the election, Mills was again drunk; and, this time he went up on stage at a strip joint where Fannie was performing (Boston's _Pilgrim Theatre_), and later held an inebriated press conference – in her dressing room! Not long after this, Mills publicly admitted to alcoholism, resigned his position, and entered a rehab facility in Florida.

Although he chose not to run for re-election in 1976, he did actively practice law at the Washington office of the prestigious New York law firm of Shea and Gould for the next 15 years. He died a year after his retirement from the law firm.

Mills and Foxe were listed by _Bloomberg_ in 2009 as the third most salacious sex scandal in US history. Just weeks after the Boston incident, she raised her weekly rate from $3,500 to $15,000.

Congressman Mills, holding one of the most sensitive positions in Congress, was found drunk, driving his car at 2:00 AM without his lights on, in the company of a neighbor who just happened to be a professional stripper and 27 years his junior, coming from a party which neither his wife nor her husband had attended, and she tried to run away from the police when they approached following the car accident. That certainly has all of the markings of a moral lapse in judgment. It also had the markings of a potentially sensitive international issue, as the stripper involved was a foreign national.

Technically, Fannie was not a stripper at the time of the accident — she had quit to be with Mills. In fact, friends of Mills reported that he and Fannie would frequently spend the night out at the *Silver Slippers* club, where she had met Mills while a dancer there. Congressman Mills even moved he and his wife into the *Crystal Towers* apartment complex in Arlington, Virginia — the apartment complex where Fannie lived with her husband.

This was not all 'discovered later'; all of this was reported in the October 11th edition of *The Washington Post*. So, how did the voters react to all this? One might expect that the incident (and the detailed account in the Post) would have been fresh in their memories on election day (which fell less than a month later); but, they appear to have forgotten all about it. They again *re-elected* Mills and returned him to the most powerful position in the US House.

Perhaps voters just don't want to buy into charges and insinuations without a criminal conviction. As the next example shows, however, even that won't necessarily ensure a rejection at the polls by the electorate.

Example #3:

Providence, RI Mayor "Buddy" Cianci

Vincent Albert "Buddy" Cianci (b. 1941) is a lawyer and radio talk show host who has served as the Mayor of Providence, Rhode Island two separate times: from 1975 to 1984, and then again from 1991 to 2002. At more than 21 years, that makes Cianci the longest serving mayor in the city's 175 year mayoral history.

After serving for 4 years as a Special Assistant Attorney General, he was appointed Prosecutor for the Rhode Island Attorney General's Anti-Corruption Strike Force. He stepped down from this when he was elected mayor in 1974. He was re-elected twice (1978 and 1982) while simultaneously (unsuccessfully) seeking Rhode Island's Governor and Senate offices. This all came to an end in 1984 when he pled *Nolo contendere* ("no contest") to assault charges. This was a felony, and Rhode Island law requires that a convicted felon step down from office. After resigning, a special election was called to replace him. Cianci tried to run to replace himself, but the Rhode Island Supreme Court ruled that the intent of the law was to prevent him either keeping the office or succeeding himself.

Cianci became a local radio talk show host, but eventually tired of that and again ran for election as mayor in 1990. Despite his felony conviction, Cianci was again elected mayor (he never lost an election until 2014). Re-elected in 1994 and again in 1998, this came to an end in 2001.

Cianci and 8 other administration officials were investigated by the FBI in an operation code-named *Operation Plunder Dome*. They were indicted in April 2001 on charges of racketeering, conspiracy, witness tampering, mail fraud, and extortion. Senior Federal District Judge Ronald Rene Lagueux said that "there is a feeling in city government in Providence that corruption is tolerated … [and, during Cianci's two terms] there has been more corruption in the City of Providence than in the history of this state."

A videotape showed a Cianci aide accepting a bribe, and Cianci publicly ridiculed the investigation. He was convicted in September

2002 of racketeering conspiracy for running a criminal enterprise, and sentenced to five years in federal prison. Convicted of a felony, Cianci was again forced to resign as mayor. At the time of his resignation, he was running unopposed for re-election to a seventh term. He appealed the conviction to the US Court of Appeals, but it was turned down. He then made a request for early release, but this was also denied.

Never one to quit, Cianci again ran for mayor in 2014, but for the first time in his career, he lost. The people of Providence may have bouts of memory loss, but even they eventually recalled what had happened.

What we have seen is the ability, the propensity, for the voters to "forget" the misdeeds of their elected officials. So far, we have seen a convicted drug abuser, an alcoholic security risk, a convicted criminal racketeer, and multiple instances of marital infidelity; however, none of these impacted the decision of the voters.

Despite these obvious lapses in memory (and judgment), we have saved the most outlandish example for last.

Example #4:

Massachusetts Governor James Michael Curley

James Michael Curley (1874–1958) served in a number of political offices: he served 4 terms as Boston mayor, 1 term as Massachusetts governor, and 2 terms in Congress. However, his political career actually began with his election to the Boston Common Council in 1900, followed by a term in the Massachusetts State House, and then to the Boston Board of Aldermen in 1904 (this form of city government was changed to a City Council in 1909). His election to the Aldermen was *while he was in prison* on a fraud conviction!

Were the voters insane? No. Were they unaware? No. Curley's conviction was for posing as someone else to take the federal civil service exam so that they could be hired by the Post Office. At this time, the Irish were a growing, but disadvantaged, slice of Boston; and, the Irish voters saw this as Curley 'looking out after his own'. Rather than forget his conviction, they remembered it when they went to the polls. They "forgot" his criminal record, but remembered his help to Boston's Irish. They re-elected Curley to the Aldermen until 1910, when Curley stepped down to run for Congress. Congressman Joseph O'Connell was seen as being in a weak position (he had won his seat by a margin of only 4 votes in 1908), so Curley ran against him in the Democratic Primary. In a three-way race, Curley won. He then won the general election in a big way in the largely Democratic district. He was re-elected in 1912, but resigned in 1914 to run for Mayor.

The Irish voters of Boston had a blank space in their memories when it came to Curley; and, as the city became increasingly Irish, more and more of the Anglo-Protestant Yankee population left Boston for the suburbs. This gave Curley a strong voter base, and he won election as the Mayor of Boston on 4 separate occasions (1914–1918, 1922–1926, 1930–1934, and 1946–1950). It appeared that, with the short Irish voter memory, Curley could do no wrong; following his third term as mayor, he was elected Governor of Massachsetts (1935 – 1937).

He was investigated and indicted for bribery and other felony charges while serving a second tour in Congress (elected in 1942 and 1944), but was again elected Mayor that Fall with the rather ironic slogan that "Curley Gets Things Done". During the campaign, a second federal grand jury added a mail fraud indictment. Curley won. At trial, he was found guilty of the charges and was sentenced to 6–18 months at the Federal Correctional Institution in Danbury, Connecticut. He remained Mayor while incarcerated,[6] with the City Clerk serving as Acting Mayor in his absence. He served 5 months of his sentence before his sentence was commuted (later, pardoned) by President Truman.

When Curley returned to Boston from prison to resume his role as mayor, a crowd of thousands greeted him at the train station — while a brass band played "Hail to the Chief". Curley made public statements that did not sit well with John Hynes (the City Clerk who had acted for him during his prison term), and Hynes effectively ended Curley's political career by running against him — and beating him — in the next 3 elections.

Curley returned to Congress in 1942 as the result of a very nasty political campaign. Running in the Democratic primary against a Roosevelt stalwart who was the son of a Unitarian minister and grandson of the President of Harvard, Curley ran a vile anti-WASP (White Anglo-Saxon Protestant) campaign that appealed to ethnic bigotry and suspicion. He even went so far as to imply in a speech that his opponent

---

6 Massachusetts, unlike Rhode Island, does not require resignation upon a felony conviction.

leaned toward the Communist Party. He easily won the election, but then voted in Congress virtually identically to the man he had just maligned and defeated.

While all of the political corruption and shenanigans were going on, Curley's personal life was a disaster. He outlived his first wife, Mary, and all but two of his 9 children. Although their electoral support eventually wavered, the Irish Catholic electorate of Boston definitely had a blind spot in their memory when it came to James Michael Curley. When he died in 1958, his funeral became one of the largest in city history.

The ability to remember past events appears to be inherent in virtually all sentient creatures — including us. Everyone has memories of things that have happened in their lives. Offer your dog a treat at noon for 5 days in a row, and you will find them sitting by the cabinet waiting for you at noon on the 6th day. This is simply the way that minds work.

Frequently, however, it does not work out this way. An *eidetic memory* (often incorrectly termed a *photographic memory*) is a very rare occurrence. Although it may appear in as much as 10% of children (although 5% is more likely), it is extraordinarily rare in adults. Bottom line: adults forget things. Their memories are not perfect, and many things "fall through the cracks". But, why is that so?

Memory loss may result from a biological failure (disease, stress, genetic, *et cetera*). It may also be the result of long periods of time having passed without recall or refresh. This is because a memory is stored in the brain cells by a chemical process. When a memory is recalled, that chemical process is apparently refreshed, so frequent recall of an event or memory may make it stronger and last longer. If the memory is never recalled over a long period of time, it may fade until it is no longer retrievable.

Another consideration is that the memory was stored in a weak manner in the first place. Something that makes a big impression on us is more likely to have a stronger chemical reaction in the brain, and more likely to be retrievable at some future point. When the event in question is routine, or lacks impact, the chemical process of storing the information in the memory may be weak;

and, as a result, this memory may not be retrievable for very long, and may not be able to be recalled with a similar degree of detail.

How does all of this apply to the collective memories of an electorate? The same processes apply in aggregate that apply in each specific person. The only real difference is the extreme improbability of a mass biological event. In other words, although an individual might suffer from a disease or genetic condition that impairs their memory, the likelihood of something like that occurring to a large segment of the population is extremely low.

It is entirely possible, however, for a significant portion of the electorate to suffer memory loss from an extended period of time having passed since an event without recall or refresh. We might expect political opponents to try to reintroduce the event in debates and advertisements so that it does not get forgotten; but, that is not always done, and even when attempted is not always successful.

The final cause offered here for memory loss was that it was originally stored in a weak manner as a result of not having made a significant impression on the voters at the time it occurred. This can result from several possible reactions to the original event:

- *they all do that* — cheating on his wife (Cora) by having sex with an ex-girlfriend? taking illegal drugs? (Marion Barry) – no big deal; they all do that.

- *not a political issue* — repeatedly getting drunk in public? having an affair with a married foreign-national stripper? (Wilbur Mills) – no big deal; those are personal issues, and not political issues (*i.e.* it shouldn't impact my vote).

- *not a big deal* — racketeering? extortion? mail fraud? misappropriation of public funds? blatant corruption? (Buddy Cianci) – stealing from the government is like stealing from an insurance company; they are constantly cheating us, so they only got what they deserved.

- *he did it for us* — forge a name on a federal civil service exam? bribery to 'grease the wheels' in Congress? accuse a loyal member of your own party of being soft on communism just to take their place in Congress? (James Curley) –

he did it for us; he helped the poor Irish and he "gets things done" (his campaign slogan) – *whatever it takes*; and, if you're Irish and poor, you have to love that.

Chapter 5
Attention Deficit

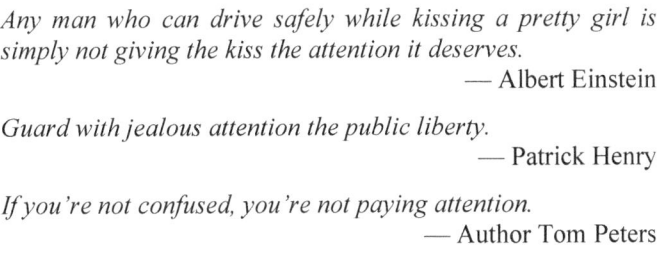

Any man who can drive safely while kissing a pretty girl is simply not giving the kiss the attention it deserves.
— Albert Einstein

Guard with jealous attention the public liberty.
— Patrick Henry

If you're not confused, you're not paying attention.
— Author Tom Peters

Patrick Henry was one of the most respected philosophers, orators, and politicians of the American revolutionary era; and, his observation that we must guard our liberty with "jealous attention" was certainly well founded. Even Einstein's observation (in the first epigraph) relates to Henry's claim, as he humorously pointed out that our attention must be totally focused in order to be successful at anything — even kissing a pretty girl.

Those sentiments certainly apply to the electoral process. To paraphrase Einstein, "anyone who can vote intelligently while worrying about personal issues is not giving their vote the attention it deserves". That clearly happens more often than it should, and has often resulted from issues such as taxation, civil rights issues, and personal freedoms.

Example #5:

US Representative Charles Diggs

Charles Coles Diggs, Jr (1922 – 1998) was an African-American who was an early activist in the American Civil Rights movement. He was elected to Congress from Michigan's 13th district in 1954, and was later selected as the first chairman of the Congressional Black Caucus (which got him a slot on Nixon's *Master List* of political opponents). He went on to be re-elected to Congress in the following 12 elections; he resigned in June of 1980 near the end of his 26th year in Congress.

Diggs was arrested and charged with mail fraud and filing false payroll forms for Congress. He was indicted and tried, and was convicted of getting kickbacks from staffers for having raised their salaries, and for 11 counts of mail fraud. He was convicted on October 7, 1978, and was awaiting sentencing when the 1978 general election took place just a month later. Despite having been found guilty of multiple felonies, he was again re-elected.

He was censured by Congress, sentenced to 3 years in prison, and resigned from Congress June 3, 1980.

Obviously, Representative Diggs was re-elected that last time because the electorate was more focused on what he might be able to do for the African-American citizenry than it was on what he had done and how he had spent their money. As Tom Peters said (third epigraph above), "if you're not confused, you're not paying attention." The voters were not confused – they wanted 'their man' in Congress. So, it can be safely assumed that they were not paying attention.

Representative Diggs, however, was not the most abusive of his public trust. Another example of where concerns trump common sense arose in the District of another of the early African-American civil rights leaders: Adam Clayton Powell (D-NY).

Example #6:

US Representative Adam Clayton Powell

Reverend Adam Clayton Powell, Jr. (1908 – 1972) was a Baptist minister and Democratic New York Congressman. He was elected to represent Harlem in Congress in 1944, and was re-elected 12 times. In 1961, he became the Chairman of the Education and Labor Committee.

Powell had been an activist on Civil Rights issues, and frequently spoke out when he saw a problem. For example, in the 1940s, Mississippi Congressman Rankin used the word "nigger" in a speech on the House floor, and Powell immediately and forcefully challenged him on it. He and Congressman William Levi Dawson (the only other black member of Congress) challenged the unwritten segregation of Capitol facilities, and he often brought black constituents with him to dine in the "Whites Only" Capitol restaurant.

For years, on every funding bill that was brought to the House floor, Powell would introduce an amendment to deny all federal funds to any district that practiced segregation. When criticized for bringing two young women with him (at Government expense) on a foreign trip, his defense was that 'everyone else was doing it'.

In 1963, the outspoken Powell was found guilty of slander and fined. He steadfastly refused to pay the judgment, and an arrest warrant was issued for him. He avoided it by spending increasing amounts of time out of state. In 1967, the House Democratic Caucus stripped him of his Chairmanship, and the full House refused to seat him until the Judiciary Committee finished its investigation of him. He was investigated for refusing to pay that NY State Court judgment in the slander case, misappropriation of Congressional travel funds, and paying his wife as a staffer for work that she never did. On March 1, 1967 the Committee reported its findings, and the House voted 307 to 116 to exclude him from his seat, and declared it vacant.

A Special Election was held to fill the vacant seat, and he ran in it to replace himself; he won. But, that would cost him his long seniority (and power), so he also sued the Speaker of the House, John McCormack. The Supreme Court ruled 7 – 1 in Powell's favor.

While the Supreme Court was hearing the case, Powell was re-elected by the voters of New York. The House, however, was not done. After he was seated for that term, the House fined Powell $25,000 and denied him seniority. The investigating committee had interviewed Powell's third wife, and she had admitted that she had been on Powell's Congressional office payroll since 1961, but that she had never done any work. In fact, she hadn't even been living in Washington — she had moved back to Puerto Rico in 1961. She was fired in 1967 when the Committee discovered this. This raises an interesting question: can you be fired from a job you never actually did?

Powell increasingly missed rollcall votes in Congress, and the voters finally had had enough. After having exercised remarkable attention deficit for years, they could no longer ignore his behavior. He was finally defeated in the Democratic primary in June of 1970, despite having told a reporter that "my people would elect me ... if I had to be propped up in my casket." Obviously, he was wrong. He contested the electoral defeat, but the recount also showed he had lost. He then resigned as pastor of the Abyssinian Baptist Church, and retired to his vacation home on the island of Bimini in the Bahamas (does anyone wonder who paid for that?).

The electorate of the district that included Harlem, New York had shown a remarkably high level of attention deficit: they had ignored Representative Powell's confrontational, arrogant manner; they had ignored his 1958 trial for tax evasion (which ended in a hung jury); they had ignored his conviction for slander for calling one of his constituents a "bag woman" for the Mafia; they had ignored his refusal to pay the $46,000 judgment awarded to her by the court; they had ignored his avoiding the arrest warrant issued for him by only returning to Harlem on Sundays to preach (since New York state law did not allow the authorities to serve a civil arrest warrant on a Sunday); they had ignored his paying his wife a salary with government funds for nearly 7 years for a job she never once did; and, they had even ignored his further misuse of Congressional funds by bringing young women with him on foreign trips. They had ignored a lot, for they believed he was their 'Congressional defender', their 'Washington advocate'. But, when he started to miss votes in Congress because he had stopped going to Washington so that he could spend more time at his vacation home in the Bahamas, they had finally had enough.

Adam Clayton Powell had been accused, and often found guilty in court, of these offenses; but, he always flat out denied them. It didn't matter to him what his constituents, his staffers, even his wife said, he denied all wrong doing.

His Congressional peer from Massachusetts, Thomas Lane, however was not so recalcitrant. When accused of wrongdoing, Lane actually pled guilty to his offenses — it didn't matter!

Example #7:

US

Representative Thomas Lane

Thomas Joseph Lane (1898 – 1994) held numerous political positions in Massachusetts — pictured above with President John F Kennedy [left], and Congressman (and future independent Presidential candidate) John B Anderson [center].

Representing the City of Lawrence, Lane served 6 terms in the Massachusetts House (from 1927 to 1938), and then 2 terms in the Massachusetts Senate (1939 to 1941). He resigned from that post when he won a special election to fill a vacant seat in the US Congress. He was then elected to a full term in 1942 and the next nine elections thereafter (serving from December 1941 to January 1963).

When Lane lost his bid for a 12th term, he turned to state politics, where he served on the Governor's Council for the Commonwealth of Massachusetts from 1965 to 1977. Nothing appears to have been able to stop the electoral successes of Thomas Lane. In 1956, after having already served all or part of 8 terms in Congress, he was re-elected after his conviction for tax fraud. He had pled guilty to tax evasion for 1949, 1950, and 1951 (avoiding an aggregate of $38,542 in income taxes), and was sentenced to 4 months in prison and a $10,000 fine. He had just been released from federal prison when he was re-elected! And, he could not claim (as did Marion Barry) that they had "set him up" because *he pled guilty!*.

That July, Lane's nomination papers had to be filed for him by his supporters because he was in jail at the time. He was released on September 4th, and then won the Democratic primary two weeks later (September 18th) with more than twice the number of votes of his nearest rival. Even more surprising was the general election, which he won in a landslide – getting more than 64% of the popular vote

---

Again, we need to ask what could lead to the public engaging in such blatant instances of "not paying attention". In the case of an individual, this is often called ADD – Attention Deficit Disorder. This is a psychologically recognized problem that begins in childhood, although the precise causes of it are not clear. Today, researchers know that there is a genetic component to ADD; but, they are not clear exactly how that manifests or how genetically controlled it is. It also appears that people with ADD suffer from an abnormal functioning of neurotransmitters in the brain.

ADHD (Attention Deficit Hyperactivity Disorder) is an umbrella term for several related disorders. There are three primary subgroups of ADHD; and, ADD, or *Inattentive ADHD*, is one of those subgroups. It is marked by significantly impaired attention and concentration. This could account for why a particular voter was "not paying attention" to what was happening; but, it could not provide a broad social explanation for an entire electorate.

Another explanation for attention deficit might be that a person's attention was focused elsewhere at the time. For example, Apollo Robbins has been described as "the greatest pickpocket in the world". He has been said to study the quirks of his target, and then use this to his advantage. To this point, one of the more common practices of a pickpocket is what is known as misdirection. The idea is to get the target to focus on something else so that the impending theft is not noticed. There are a number of ways that this can be done. For example:

- *Sandwiching* — one person stops abruptly in front of you, causing you to bump into them; a second person bumps into you as you stop, and the confusion allows the second person to pick your pocket.

- *Pressuring* — somebody trips and grabs your shoulder to keep from falling to the ground; the pressure on your shoulder keeps you from noticing that they are simultaneously picking your pocket.

- *Startling* — a loud noise or clatter causes you to shift your attention to what caused the noise, and the pickpocket takes that opportunity to take what they want.

- *Distracting* — a group of children (in the author's personal experience, it was a group of elderly women in Italy) crush around you and cause confusion and distraction while one of them attempts to pick your pocket.

Finally, we have the situation where there is something that has a person thoroughly engrossed in a subject, and extraneous events simply do not carry sufficient weight to warrant their full attention. Any wife who has tried to talk to their husband about dinner during a televised football game knows exactly what I am describing here.

The problem, as it was with memory loss, is that all of these are not easily transferred to a large social grouping. Although an individual, or even several related family members may suffer from ADD, that is not something that can, or ever has, impacted an entire cultural grouping such as an electorate. The other two, however, could.

For example misdirection, regardless of which form it takes, can apply not only to individuals, but also to large groups. There was a successful movie released in 1997 that starred Dustin Hoffman and Robert De Niro called *Wag the Dog*. The story line was that a political operative hired a film producer to "invent" a fake war with Albania. The reason for this was to distract the public from a brewing sex scandal only days before the presidential election.

Coincidentally, the film was released just a month before the Monica Lewinsky scandal broke into the headlines during the Clinton administration. The following August, President Clinton ordered a cruise missile strike on the al-Shifa Pharmaceutical factory in Khartoum, Sudan. Although the government gave several possible alternative reasons for the strike, the media (as well as a number of foreign governments) disputed the claims made about the factory. It was probably inevitable that the media quickly compared the Lewinsky Affair and al-Shifa attack to the movie. Whatever the real reason for the strike, it certainly did refocus the American attention – just as it did in the movie.

Another case is when our focus is so directed on a single area that we tend to overlook what is happening elsewhere. During World War II, the US was so focused on working with the Allies to defeat Hitler that it ignored the actions of the Soviet Union.

Even though the existence of Comintern (the *Communist International*) had been discovered by the US to have been illegally funding the US Communist Party (CPUSA) during the 1920s and 1930s, the US nevertheless undertook the *Lend-Lease Program* during the 1940s (from March 1941 to September 1945). This was a program where the United States gave food, oil, and materiel (commercial and military hardware and equipment) to Great Britain, Free France, the Republic of China, and the Soviet Union. The total cost of the program was just over $50 billion, of which $11.3 billion went to the Soviet Union. Considering what we had learned about Comintern illegally funding the CPUSA, why would the US provide the Soviet Union with over $11 billion in supplies? *Attention Deficit*. The US was distracted; our attention was elsewhere; our biggest concern at the time was the defeat of Nazi Germany. The result was that our attention (and our actions) were not focused on what the Soviet Union had done, was doing, or would likely be doing in the future.

We also see "startling distractions" in the world at large. For example, when the twin towers at the World Trade Center in New York City were attacked on September 11, 2001, this was, to put it mildly, startling to the American public. Absolutely nothing was getting the public's full attention in the days and weeks that followed. The sudden events of that morning completely dominated the media and the public.

We can see all of these same distraction processes taking place in the electorate in many elections.

- *Pressuiring* — in the 1992 US Presidential election, the Democratic candidate (William Jefferson "Bill" Clinton) worked constantly to keep pressure on the election. That pressure was summarized in an expression coined by his campaign strategist, James Carville. That expression, it's "the economy, stupid" was instrumental in having his opponent's job approval rating drop from 89% (February 28, 1991) to 29% (July 31, 1992) — a 60% drop in just 17 months. That drop – impacted heavily by the pressure that kept the electorate from paying attention to anything else – led directly to the electorate rejecting a second term for President George H W Bush.

- *Startling* — President George W Bush had an average job approval rating of 49.4% over his 8 years in office. However, the startling events of September 11th so distracted the electorate from anything else that his job approval simply exploded. On the evening of September 20, 2001, he addressed the American public and a joint session of the 107th Congress. The next day saw his approval at 90%. As long as he said the right things about the terrorist attack, it really didn't matter what else he might do — nobody was paying attention.

- *Distracting* — on November 4, 1979, 52 Americans were taken hostage in Tehran, Iran. The hostages were held by the Iranians for more than a year. This had a very negative impact on the 1980 election. So long as the hostages were in Iranian custody, President James Earl "Jimmy" Carter appeared weak and ineffective. His opponent, Republican Ronald Reagan, talked tough and kept attention on the hostage crisis. The electorate responded and elected Reagan. Exactly 20 minutes after Reagan's inaugural address, the Islamic Republic of Iran released the hostages. Conspiracy theories quickly arose that claimed Reagan's campaign had promised Iran weapons (funneled through Israel) and a release of frozen Iranian assets in return for delaying the release of the hostages. Reagan denied this, and there was no proof that any such agreement existed. However, then-Israeli Prime Minister Yitzhak Shamir, then-Iranian President Abolhassan Banisadr, National Security Council member Gary Sick, and Reagan campaign staffer Barbara Honegger all insisted it was true. Whether it was planned or coincidental, the continuing hostage crisis so distracted the electorate that nothing else got any attention.

The reason is not really of tremendous concern; and, the method used to ensure it is not terribly important. What is important is that the electorate is distracted so that they are not "paying attention" to what has been happening. All too often, that is a common electoral campaign tactic.

Chapter 6

Ignorance

Anti-intellectualism has been a constant thread winding its way through our political and cultural life, nurtured by the false notion that democracy means that "my ignorance is just as good as your knowledge."   — Isaac Asimov

The best argument against democracy is a five-minute conversation with the average voter.   — Winston Churchill

Sometimes, elections go wrong for the worst of all possible reasons: the electorate is just plain stupid! Well, technically, that is inaccurate. *Stupid* is a term that is most often defined as "lack of intelligence". A more accurate term would be *ignorance*, which is best defined as a "lack of information". It is entirely feasible to have intelligent people who simply lack the information necessary to make an intelligent decision. So, they are not so much "stupid" as "ignorant". And, we have lots of examples where the electorate was apparently totally ignorant.

Ignorance, however, does not mean that the electorate (or even a solitary voter) needs to be uninformed about *everything*, but only that there are specific facts of which they lack any real knowledge. For example, consider the fact that an individual politician is guilty of embezzling money from government funds which they oversee. This may not negatively impact an impending election for several possible reasons:

- *Memory Loss* — we have already seen examples of what can happen when the electorate "forgets" that this embezzlement has occurred. This might occur if the embezzlement had happened years earlier at a time when the electorate was differently constituted, or had been so long ago that it was merely a "distant memory".

- *Attention Deficit* — this can result from the electorate being so focused on something else that they paid no attention to the revelation of the embezzlement. This could happen, for example, if the embezzler's opponent had been caught by the national news media in a very salacious situation. The prurient interests of the electorate may preclude their paying any attention to something so "dull" as theft.

- *Ignorance* — the embezzlement may not be revealed until after the polls have closed, so that the electorate was completely ignorant of the crime until <u>after</u> they had already cast their vote.

In our first example, we have a candidate often considered – but, at that point, <u>not</u> <u>yet</u> <u>proven</u> – to be corrupt. He even had his Congressional office raided by the FBI, and still won re-election six months later. The electorate, however, was not yet convinced of either the severity of his alleged crimes, the indictment that would follow 7 months after the election, or the conviction it would eventually produce. They were, in a word, *ignorant*.

Example #8:

US Representative William "Bill" Jefferson

William Jennings "Bill" Jefferson (b. 1947) was a legislative assistant in the US Senate from 1973 to 1975, and then moved to New Orleans to pursue his own policial career. He was elected to the Louisiana State Senate in 1979, and was continuously re-elected until he resigned in 1990 in the middle of his 3rd four-year term. Twice during this time in office, he ran for Mayor of New Orleans, but lost both times. It was during the first of these attempts (1982) that his opponent, incumbent mayor Dutch Morial, coined a nickname for Jefferson that he has had ever since: "Dollar Bill".

In 1990, the incumbent 10-term Representative from the 2nd Louisiana Congressional district announced her retirement, and Jefferson decided to run for her seat. He won, and was continuously re-elected — serving from 1991 until he was finally defeated in a run-off election in 2008. Subsequent re-elections were usually by a landslide of more than 75%. While in Congress, Jefferson ran for Governor in 1999, but was soundly defeated.

Jefferson controlled one of the most effective "get out the vote" operations anywhere – using it to promote friends, relatives, and protégés to office in Louisiana; for example:
- Renée Pratt (protégée) – New Orleans City Council (2002)
- Jalila Jefferon-Bullock (daughter) – State House (2005)
- Barbara "Betty" Jefferson Jackson (sister) – Municipal Assessor, New Orleans 4th District (1998, 2002, …)
- Mose Oliver Jefferson (brother) – street lieutenant for the *Progressive Democrats*.

In May of 2006, the FBI raided Jefferson's Congressional office looking for evidence of bribery. Although he was re-elected 6 months later, the Democratic leader in the US House (Nancy Pelosi) informed him that he would not be allowed to resume his Committee appointments until the Federal probe was completed. The following June, he was indicted by a federal grand jury on 16 corruption-related charges.

Congressman Jefferson was convicted on 11 of the 16 charges. His brother and sister were later brought up on related bribery and obstruction of justice charges. Although Betty (his sister) died before a final judgment, Mose (his brother) was found guilty on 4 charges. Both Mose and Betty are now deceased.

Jefferson was ordered to serve a 13 year prison sentence for the 11 felonies for which he was convicted. He appealed, and one of the eleven convictions was overturned; but, the other 10 were confirmed. He began serving his sentence on May 4, 2012. It is the longest prison sentence ever given to a member of Congress for any crime.

The electorate of the 2nd District had had plenty of opportunities to see what "Dollar Bill" Jefferson was like:
- his reputation for corruption was well enough known that he was nicknamed *Dollar Bill* as early as 1982;
- his *Progressive Democrats* political machine regularly promoted Jefferson's nepotistic candidates;
- in 2005, a few days after Hurrican Katrina devastated Louisiana, Jefferson diverted National Guard troops from aiding the homeless and injured to recover items from his house for him; when the National Guard truck (with troops and Jefferson aboard) got stuck in the mud, he had a National Guard helicopter delay rescue operations to come get them and complete the recovery; and,
- that same year (July 30), the FBI videotaped Jefferson accepting a $100,000 bribe; and, 4 days later, they raided his home in Washington DC and found $90,000 of it wrapped in aluminum foil hidden in his freezer;

- in January 2006, a Jefferson aide (Brett Pfeffer) pled guilty to conspiracy and aiding in the bribery of a Congressman; and,
- later that year, the FBI raided Jefferson's Congressional office to gather the evidence to formally charge him.

All of this happened <u>before</u> Jefferson's 2006 re-election with 56.6% of the vote. And, in the unusual Louisiana electoral system, his re-election was not based on either race or political party: the opponent he defeated in the December run-off election was also African-American and Democrat (Karen Carter).

It was not until 2008 that Jefferson – an African-American Democrat running in a largely African-American Democratic district – finally lost the support of the electorate. But, even when facing an impending trial on 16 felony indictments and massive media coverage of the evidence, he still only lost re-election by 3 percentage points, while in that same elction, President Barack Obama received 72% of the vote — in Jefferson's district!

Was the 2nd Louisiana Congressional District electorate really that ignorant of who they were re-electing? As said before the review of Jefferson''s story, the electorate "was <u>not</u> <u>yet</u> <u>aware</u> of either the severity of his alleged crimes, the indictment that would follow 7 months after the election, or the conviction it would eventually produce." Although that is all true, those 6 points listed above make it perfectly clear that perhaps they <u>should</u> have known what he was like.

Another example of electorate ignorance involves not corrupttion, but blatant, racist activism. This example comes from a state that is:

- 40% WASP (White Anglo-Saxon Protestant)
- 32% African-American
- 28% Roman Catholic
- 5% Hispanic
- 2¼% Asian-American
- 2% Muslim, Buddhist or Jewish

These percentages are important because – with the obvious exception of the 40% minority that are white Protestants – these are all ethnic or religious groups that this individual had actively opposed and demeaned.

Example #9:

Louisiana State Representative David Duke

David Ernest Duke (b. 1950) is a white supremacist writer, politician, neo-Nazi, Holocaust revisionist, and white separatist. He is also a former Grand Dragon of the Ku Klux Klan. In fact, after joining the KKK as a teenager in 1967, he founded a "more professional" group, the *Knights of the KKK*, in 1974. While attending LSU, he would often attend classes and walk around campus wearing a Nazi uniform.

Duke left the Knights of the KKK in 1980 to found another white supremacist group, the *National Association for the Advancement of White People* (NAAWP). Duke has been a frequent candidate for political office:

- 1975 – Louisiana State Senate (lost, but got 33% of the vote)
- 1979 – Louisiana State Senate (again lost, but with 26% of the vote)
- 1988 – Louisiana Democratic Primary for President (came in 6th, with more than 23,000 votes)
- 1988 – President of the United States (lost – received 47,000 votes)
- 1989 – Louisiana State Representative (won, with 51% of the vote)
- 1990 – US Senate (lost with 43% of the vote — 607,000 votes)
- 1991 – Louisiana Governor (lost, with 39% of the vote — 671,000)
- 1992 – Louisiana Republican Primary for President (came in 3rd, with about 12,000 votes)
- 1996 – US Senate (lost, but got 141,489 votes)
- 1999 – US Representative (came in 3rd with 28,000 votes — missed runoff by just 3,000 votes)

In 1988, Duke won the first election in his long career. Running in the 1988 Democratic Presidential primaries was generally a disaster; but, he did win the Vice-Presidential Primary in New Hampshire. Getting discouraged by his lack of success in the Democratic presidential primaries, he decided to pursue the nomination of the small Populist Party; he got it, and got 47,000 votes.

The Populist Party was on the ballot in just 11 states, but also ran a write-in campaign in several others. The FEC recorded 47,047 votes cast for Duke for President. After losing, he switched his formal party affiliation from the Democrats to the Republicans the following month.

Early the next year, a Louisiana Republican State Rep (Charles Cusimano) resigned to become a Judicial District Court Judge. Duke ran in the special election, and finished 1st with 33% of the vote. In the run-off election, Duke's opponent (fellow Republican John Treen) was endorsed by the President (GHW Bush), the former President (Ronald Reagan), several national Republicans, and even the Democratic head of the Louisiana AFL-CIO. The people elected Duke anyway, with 51% of the vote.

Duke has often accused Jews of controlling the Federal Reserve System, the mass media, and virtually all of the Federal Government. He has praised the Nazis, denied the Holocaust, and founded multiple white racist groups. In 2005, he received a "Candidate of Sciences" degree from the Interregional Academy of Personnel Management. This school is reportedly the largest source of anti-Semitic literature in Ukraine; and, Duke's thesis was titled "Zionism as a Form of Ethnic Supremacism". Ever since being awarded this degree, Duke refers to himself as David Duke, PhD.

In 2009, he was arrested in the Czech Republic for violating their laws regarding promoting Nazi Germany and the Holocaust. Four years later, Duke was expelled from his home in Italy when they discovered that he had been banned from the 26 country Schengen Area (effectively nearly all of Western Europe) by Switzerland.

David Duke has been largely a failure as a politician – losing about 10 times as many elections as he has won. He has been branded as a pariah by more than two dozen countries. He has flaunted his dislike, distrust, and hatred for Jews, Blacks, Asians, and nearly every minority group in either Louisiana or the United States as a whole. He wrote a self-help book (1976) for women that recommended fellatio, anal sex, and vaginal exercises. His autobiography (*My Awakening*) is replete with blatant racial overtones. The Anti-Defamation League calls it racist, sexist, homophobic, and anti-Semitic (*i.e.* they didn't like it).

David Duke, to put it mildly, is an interesting case in point for this section. What, except for blatant ignorance, could account for the number of votes he has received in numerous elections? He has long campaigned for, and spoken out on, issues to the clear detriment of African-Americans, Jews, Asian-Americans, Hispanics, and Roman Catholics. He lost a run for the US Senate with 43% of the vote in a state where only 40% of the voters are White Anglo-Saxon Protestants (about the only group Duke has not insulted). The following year, he lost the governorship with 39% of the vote. If the voters were not ignorant of what Duke has stood for his entire life, then what in the world were they thinking?

Finally, we have the case of a Federal District Judge impeach-ed by the US House of Representatives. Impeachment, however, is comparable to an indictment; it does not signify a finding of actual guilt – it signifies a finding that there is sufficient reason to suspect guilt that an actual trial is warranted. Under US law, this trial is then conducted by the US Senate. In this case, the Senate determined there was actual guilt, and he was convicted by the Sen-ate, and removed from office. After losing his appeal to the Supreme Court (his conviction and removal were confirmed), he decided to run for elected office. He ran for Congress in the next election! After all, if the justice system has seen the wisdom of throwing you out of office, perhaps the voters will be kinder. They were: apparently the electorate must have been totally ignorant of the events that had involved him as a judge, and overwhelmingly elected him to Congress.

Example #10:

US Representative Alcee Hastings

Alcee Lamar Hastings (b. 1936) has been the US Representative from southeastern Florida for the past 22 years. He was elected from the 23rd Congressional District in 1993 – a district that ran from Saint Lucie County in the north and took in large parts of Martin, Hendry, Palm Beach, and Broward counties. Redistricting caused by the 2010 Census put him in the 20th Congressional District, which is a little fur-ther south, and runs down to Miami. He also won in this new District.

Alcee Hastings was a Circuit Court Judge from 1977; but, after 2 years, President Carter appointed him as US District Court Judge for the Southern District of Florida in 1979. His term was not uneventful: in 1981, he was charged with accepting a $150,000 bribe in return for a lenient sentence and a return of assets seized in a racketeering case. In 1983, he was acquitted largely because his co-conspirator refused to testify. His problems, though, did not end with the acquittal. In 1988, the US House of Representatives impeached Judge Hastings on a 413-3 rollcall vote. This was not a case of bitter partisan politics: despite the fact that Hastings was a Democrat, and the US House was solidly Democratic (258–177), 99.3% of the House voted to impeach. The following year, he was tried by the US Senate. The Senate was also solidly Democratic (55–45), and conviction required a guilty vote by two-thirds of the Senators. If found guilty of a single charge, it would get him removed from office. He was found guilty on 8 of the charges.

The Senate had voted on 11 of the charges brought by the House, and a majority voted guilty on 10 of them. On two charges, however, they failed to get the two-thirds required to convict. Hastings filed a case in Federal Court to challenge the Senate actions, but the Supreme Court ruled against him, and his expulsion stood. As such, he is only one of eight federal officials in US history to be impeached, convicted, and removed from office (not an enviable "accomplishment").

While awaiting a decision from the Supreme Court, Hastings decided to run for elective office. So, in 1992, he ran in the Democratic primary for the US House from Florida's 23rd District. He placed second in the Democratic primaries for the post, but no candidate had a clear majority. In the runoff primary, Hastings scored what many considered to be an upset victory over State Representative Lois Frankel, who had initially placed first. He went on to easily win election in the final election. He has repeatedly won re-election; and, even following redistricting (in the 2012 election), Hastings continues to win. He now represents Florida's 20th Congressional district.

In 2012, a ranking of US House members on the basis of how much they paid in salaries and fees to family members ranked Hastings as #1 out of 435 Congressmen. *Ciizens for Responsibility and Ethics in Washington* reported that, for the four years from 2007 to 2010, Hastings had even paid his girlfriend $622,574.

When Hastings came up for his first re-election campaign in his new 20th Congressional District on November 4, 2014, he was challenged in the Democratic Primary by Palm Beach Port Commissioner Jean Enright and former heavyweight boxer Jameel McCline. Hastings won the primary, and went on to face Republican Jay Bonner in the general election. Hastings won the election with 81.6% of the vote (128,498 to 28,968)!

What could account for these brief examples (there are many, many more)? Repeatedly elect and re-elect a nepotistic crook? Vote for a racist bigot who is biased against you? Consider a US District Court Judge impeached by the US House of Representatives, convicted by the US Senate, and permanently removed from the bench by the US Supreme Court, and decide that he would be a good Congressman? The possible reasons are really limited to just two: stupidity or ignorance. We already decided that stupidity is not something with which we can brand an entire electorate; so, the only possibility is *ignorance*!

Chapter 7

Greed

Well first of all, tell me: Is there some society you know that doesn't run on greed? ... Of course, none of us are greedy, it's only the other fellow who's greedy. The world runs on individuals pursuing their separate interests.
— Milton Friedman (economist)

In a society governed passively by free markets and free elections, organized greed always defeats disorganized democracy. — Matthew C. Taibbi (author)

Advocates of capitalism are very apt to appeal to the sacred principles of liberty, which are embodied in one maxim: The fortunate must not be restrained in the exercise of tyranny over the unfortunate. — Bertrand Russell

Capitalism tries for a delicate balance: It attempts to work things out so that everyone gets just enough stuff to keep them from getting violent and trying to take other people's stuff.
— George Carlin

Greed may be a little on the aggressive side for naming this particular reason for the electorate sometimes doing really foolish things; other, less aggressive terms for this might include desire, financial motivation, or monetary gain. Of course, economist Milton Friedman (long time Economics Professor at the University of Chicago) had no problem calling it greed (1st epigraph above); but, he was not being critical. He saw greed as an essential motivating force in a free market economy.

Author Matthew Taibbi has a much more negative view of the role of greed — pointing out that "organized greed always defeats disorganized democracy" (2nd epigraph). This is actually what we are exploring in this chapter: the idea that organized, structured financial schemes often seem to derail a disorganized, unstructured democracy.

Bertrand Russell, the British philosopher, was rather blunt (as was his usual approach) — pointing out that active capitalists often base their arguments on the sacrosanct principle of liberty: that it would be a despotic act to deny the fortunate (or, as Karl Marx called them, the "haves") the freedom to run roughshod over the unfortunate (*i.e.* the "have nots"). This is often exactly what occurs when wealthy patrons fund compliant politicians with extravagant sums to conduct their campaigns.

Perhaps the most accurate assessment, however, comes — as it so often does — from comedian George Carlin. He said (in the 4th epigraph) that the real goal of capitalism is to find that point where these unfortunates manage to get just enough of the economic pie that they do not erupt in a violent, forceful revot agains those who are getting nearly everything —no more; just enough.

Example #11:

Political Party Allegiance by Income

In political circles, it has long been an "urban myth" that wealthy people vote Republican, while the destitute and poor vote Democrat. The implication is that the Republicans are the party of the rich and successful, while the Democrats are the party of the indigent. This is more than just a myth, however, as polling data lends some credence to these views.

Professor Paul Robin Krugman (Profesor of Economics and International Affairs at Princeton) has documented polls from 2006 that showed an interesting break at $100,000 income: 55% of those making less than this voted Democratic, while 52% making more voted Republican. This is not a huge difference; but, the balance definitely swings Republican when that income level is passed. Krugman also noted that this trend has been reported since at least the early 1970s.

When income rises to above $200,000, the percentage voting Republican rises to 63%. And, the exact opposite is true as income levels decline. The exact same percentage (63%) vote Democratic when their income drops below $15,000.

Although economics is a major factor, it is not the only demographic difference between the parties – although some of these other differences relate indirectly to finances. In polls conducted as recently as 2012, 87% of Republican voters are white, while that number drops to 61% among Democrats. Amongst Democrats, 21% are African-American, 10% are Hispanic, and 7% report they are another racial minority. By contrast, only 11% of Republicans are a minority *of any grouping!*

There is also a party preference by gender. Although 50% of the US population between 15 and 64 is male (it drops to 48% when the very young and very old are included), Republicans are 52% male while only 43% of Democrats are male.

Educationally, the Pew Forum has identified that 52% of college graduates identify as Democrat or "leaning Democrat", while only 40% identify as Republican or "leaning Republican". When only those with graduate college degrees are considered, the imbalance jumps to 56% *vs.* 36%. In other words, the best educated American voters are more than 50% more likely to vote Democrat than Republican.

Again considering income only, the shift between parties can clearly be seen as income levels change:

Income Level	% Republican	% Democrat
Below $20,000	29	40
$20,000 – $30,000	33	34
$30,000 – $50,000	40	28
$50,000 – $75,000	43	26
$75,000 – $100,000	45	25

As the income bracket kept rising, the % that vote Republican kept rising; and, as income rose, the % that vote Democrat kept dropping. This can also be seen in the answer to two questions asked in a 2012 "do you agree?" poll:

Our society should do what is necessary to make sure that everyone has an equal opportunity to succeed.

Republicans	74% Agree	22% Disagree
Democrats	94% Agree	4% Disagree

We have gone too far in pusing equal rights in this country.

Republicans	61% Agree	33% Disagree
Democrats	27% Agree	72% Disagree

There is a great deal of raw data in that last example (#11); so, how can we "make sense" of it? Republican policies have, since 1980, been based in large part on the policies of President Ronald Reagan. Reagan, in turn, was basing many of his policies on the position of Arizona Senator Barry M Goldwater (the Republican candidate for President in 1964). Economically, these policies tend to push lower taxes, more unbridled capitalism, and a meritocracy approach to personal success. These policies are clearly more appealing to those with large incomes (where lower taxes have a much greater impact), greater liquid assets (where a truly free and unrestricted economy offers more opportunities), and greater wealth (since this would imply greater merit — *i.e.* they "earned" it).

By contrast, the Democratic Party has, since the 1930s, pushed policies requiring higher taxes, more government involvement in the lives of its citizens, and an implied "social contract" to look out after those who have not done as well as others. Again, it should not be a surprise that these policies are more appealing to those with limited income (where higher taxes are largely shielded by deductions that protect the poor), fewer assets (where government involvement and assistance is virtually required for medical care, retirement, and other necessities of life), and little if any "wealth" (where this social contract, or safety net, is all that stands between them and abject poverty).

So, is it "greed" that generally has the poorest voting Democratic, and the wealthy voting Republican? Not really. But, there is definitely a "financial motivation" for each of them. And, this can often get them to ignore other factors when deciding how to cast their ballot.

Example #12:

US Senator Robert Byrd
(*born Cornelius Calvin Sale, Jr.*)

Robert Carlyle Byrd (1917– 2010) was born as Cornelius Calvin Sale, Jr. (he was adopted by his aunt and uncle, who changed his name, after his mother died in the 1918 flu pandemic when he was just 10 months old). He served as the US Representative for West Virginia's 6th Congressional District from 1953 to 1959 (3 terms: the 83rd, 84th, and 85th Congresses). He left the House in 1959 to run for the Senate, and was elected, and then re-elected 8 times. At his death in 2010, he was the longest serving member of Congress in US hitory – a record that would be eclipsed by Representative John Dingell 2 years later (D-Michigan, serving 59 years starting in 1955, and retiring in 2015).

Senator Byrd had been a member, recruiter, and leader within the Ku Klux Klan in the 1940s, but left to pursue politics. He was a powerful member of the Senate, and served as the Senate Minority Leader during the Reagan administration (1981 – 1987), and as President *pro tempore* of the Senate between 1989 and 2010 whenever Democrats held the majority, and as President *pro tempore emeritus* whenever Republicans held the majority. This role actually put him 3rd in line for the presidency after the Vice-President and Speaker of the House. As Chairman of the Senate Appropriations Committee (1989–1995, 2001–2003, and 2007–2009), he had tremendous influence over federal spending.

Byrd used his influence in the Appropriations Committee to funnel disproportionate amounts of federal money to projects back in his home state of West Virginia. His critics were highly critical of this spending, but the people in West Virginia were appreciative – with their votes.

Byrd had left the Ku Klux Klan prior to entering national politics; however, he had been unanimously elected to the top officer's position in his local chapter (Exalted Cyclops), and it was a Klan official that convinced a young Robert Byrd to enter politics. He ran for the West Virginia House of Delegates in 1946 and served from 1947 to 1950. He was then elected to the West Virginia Senate for 1951 and 1952. About a dozen years later, Byrd would use his position in the US Senate to filibuster against the passage of the Civil Rights Act of 1964. In 1946, Byrd had even written a letter to Mississippi Senator Bilbo that said "I shall never fight in the armed forces with a negro by my side … I should die a thousand times, and see Old Glory trampled in the dirt never to rise again, than to see this beloved land of ours become degraded by race mongrels".

Although Byrd claimed to have left the Klan after only a year, and had not been involved for the 9 years prior to his campaign for the House in 1952, he wrote that letter to Senator Bilbo in 1946, and had also written to the KKK Grand Wizard in 1947 that said he thought "the Klan is needed today as never before, and I am anxious to see its rebirth here in West Vrginia and in every state in the nation."

Although it appears that Byrd was either active in, or supported, the Klan for much longer than he publicly acknowledged, he did eventually change his views. In 2005, at the age of 88, Byrd said "I know now I was wrong. Intolerance had no place in America. I apologized a thousand times … and I don't mind apologizing over and over again. I can't erase what happened."

> West Virginia is one of the "whitest" states in the US (94%–16%;
> higher than the US in total), and most English-speaking (only 2.4%
> speak something else at home, where 20.7% do for the US). Only 3.6%
> of the population is Black (about ¼ the national average).

There can really be no legitimate argument that Senator Robert Byrd was not a racist. And, West Virginia is historically one of the whitest states in the entire country. But, that was not what typically got Byrd re-elected to office with pluralities of 59% to 78% (one election, 1976, he got 100% – the Republicans didn't even bother to field a candidate to run against him). What got him elected, re-elected, and re-elected again was *greed!* Byrd funneled huge amounts of federal money into West Virginia during his years in the Senate.

There are statues to Byrd; bas reliefs of him; two highway interchanges named for him; a bridge, dam, locks, two courthouses with his name; a $75 million radio telescope complex; four stretches of highway; the Hardwood Technology Center; the Health and Wellness Center; the Institute for Advanced Flexible Manufacturing; the Lifelong Learning Center; and more than two dozen other federally funded grants to West Virginia. The Senator, when re-elected to his 8th Senate term in 2000, told his supporters that "West Virginia has always had four friends: God Almighty, Sears Roebuck, Carter's Liver Pills and Robert C. Byrd". Just 10 years earlier, he had said "I want to be West Virginia's billion-dollar industry". He was; and, the voters of West Virginia recognized that and kept returning him to the Senate.

There might have been problems with Senator Byrd (racism, narcissism, opinionated, obsessive, *et cetera*); but, he sent money and jobs — lots of money, and lots of jobs — to West Virginia. And, the voters of West Virginia, ensuring their own best financial interests, made sure that Byrd stayed in Washington where he could ensure that would continue — in 64 years of elected, public service, Senator Robert C. Byrd *never* lost an election!

Example #13:

US Representative Jack Murtha

John Patrick "Jack" Murtha, Jr. (1932–2010) represented the 12th Congressional District in Pennsylvania for 36 years. After serving in the Pennsylbania House for 5 years, Murtha ran in a special election in 1974 for the US House of Representatives; he won, and held the office through 18 Congresses. He was the first Viet Nam veteran elected to the US House; and, as a former Marine Corps officer, his opinion on military issues was often given significant credence.

His terms in Congress were not without controversy, however. In their 2005 report, CREW (*Citizens for Responsibility and Ethics in Washington*) labeled him one of the 20 most currupt members of Congress; and, the following year, they branded him as one of the "Five Members to Watch". They were concerned about his steering of defense appropriations to clients of KSA Consulting (where his brother worked) and PMA Group (founded by a former staffer). In 2008, *Esquire* magazine named him as one of the 10 worst members of Congress, based in large part on his opposition to ethics reforms and his funnelling of $100 million a year of federal defense spending into his district. A local newpaper praised him for his ability to "cross the aisle" to deliver pork (inflated spending) to his district.

In the 2008 Defense appropriations spending bill (which Murtha oversaw as Chairman of the House Appropriations Subcommittee on Defense), more than $38 million was directed to clients of PMA Group. The following Spring (March 2009), the *Washington Post* reported that a Pennsylvania defense research center frequently consulted with Murtha staffers while receiving almost a quarter of a billion dollars in earmarked federal defense spending. They then forwarded a significant portion of that funding to companies that had supported Murtha's election campaigns.

In 1980, Murtha was implicated in the Abscam scandal. Abscam was an undercover FBI sting investigation into bribery of public officials. It began as an investigation into the handling of stolen property, and the corruption of legitimate businessmen; but, it soon evolved into an investigation of public corruption – investigating the offer of bribes to public officials in return for political favors.

Among others, 6 US Congressmen and 1 US Senator were convicted in the Abscam investigation. Murtha was not among these, but he was listed as an "unindicted co-conspirator". In the investigation, FBI agents posed as contacts for Saudi Arabians who supposedly wanted to use bribes to facilitate immigration into the US. Murtha did meet with these contacts, and the FBI videotaped his meeting on a hidden camera. To his credit, Murtha told the contacts that "I'm not interested." Despite this, he apparently left the door open, by telling them that if "we do business for a while, maybe I'll be interested, maybe I won't". Murtha did, however, provide the names of businesses and financial institutions back in his home district where the Saudis could legally invest money. Although this money might later be used to bribe US officials, the US Attorney determined that Murtha's goal was to get them to use banks in his district as opposed to somewhere else. He even told them that these investments could easily result in putting up to a thousand out-of-work miners in his district back to work.

Murtha was not charged; but, he did agree to testify on behalf of the government against two fellow Congressmen (John Murphy of New York, and Frank Thompson of New Jersey). These two had also been at the meeting with the contacts, had agreed to participate, and were later filmed putting the bribes in their pockets.

Jack Murtha was apparently not inherently dishonest. He turned down a $50,000 offer from the undercover FBI agents, and never did accept any money; however, he was not squeaky clean, either. He recommended investment opportunities in his district where he knew, or should have known, that bribe money might be "laundered" by legal institutions.

This all happened near the start of Murtha's 4th term in Congress; and, the media gave extensive national coverage to the Abscam Investigation — after all, 6 US Congressmen, a US Senator, an INS Supervisor, and others were all convicted in court. Nonetheless, the voters of Pennsylvania's 12th Congressional District returned Murtha to Congress 14 more times. Why?

Greed. Jack Murtha spent years on the Defense Subcommittee of the Appropriations Committee — the people who decided which Department of Defense projects would be funded, and where that money would go. Murtha was in a unique position to help the people of his district, and he did so relentlessly. As Chairman of that

Subcommittee, he channeled about $100 million dollars each year into his home district. Using a very rough calculation, if half of that money went into supplies and materials, while the other half went for labor (assuming an average labor cost of ~$50,000 per year per person), Murtha was providing his district with about a thousand well paid jobs every year. That is also what Murtha thought that the Abscam money might provide in his district.

So, it apparently wasn't personal greed that motivated Jack Murtha; and, it evidently wasn't personal dishonesty (although we could argue that what he did was fundamentally dishonest, as it cheated the people of the other 434 Congressional Districts). What Murtha did was to put money and jobs back into his District; and, the voters of his district responded with a resounding and repeated "ThankYou" at the polls.

Not all instances of financial motivation are as clear as the cases of Senator Byrd and Representative Murtha; but, that does not mean that the voters' personal "best interests" don't frequently factor into their decisions. As was pointed out in Example #11, the two predominant political parties inherently appeal to different economic strata within society: Republicans appealing more to the wealthier, while Democrats appeal more to the less affluent.

The problem is that neither group – the wealthy, nor the poor – is numerous enough to elect a candidate on their own. They each need a significant number of voters from what can humorously be called the "middle class". It is humorous because it is a "class" that is rapidly disappearing, if it ever actually existed at all.

Income inequality in a capitalist economy is to be expected; it is even to be desired. It is the promise of gain that motivates ambition, creativity, and dedication. Financial gain is the reward for having worked hard, taken chances, and sacrificed. However, in the United States, the disparity between the wealthiest and the poorest among us is currently greater than it has ever been at any point in human history, in any corner of the globe. And, this is occurring as the middle class is either rising into the wealthier strata, or being dragged down into the poorer strata. The "true" middle class – those that work hard and live a relatively comfortable, secure life – is slowly, but steadily, disappearing.

According to the pollster Gallup, 63% of Americans consider-ed themselves "middle class" when President George W Bush took office in 2001. That number had dropped to 51% by 2015 (after a nearly even mix of Republican and Democratic administrations, so it does not imply that either party is directly responsible). By con-trast, 33% of Americans considered themselves "working or lower class" back in 2001, and that rose to 48% by 2015.

In 2015, 63% of the public believes that wealth should be more evenly distributed in society, while 31% believe that the current distribution is fair. Even as 19% of the middle class believed that they had dropped out of the middle class into the lower class, and the size of the lower class had jumped by 45%, the number that thought that wealth distribution was "fair" didn't change: 31% think it is fair in 2015, while the exact same 31% thought so back at the start of the second Reagan administration (1985). The 63% that think wealth should be more evenly distributed only rose slightly from the 60% who thought so back in 1985.

The challenge for the Democratic Party is to convince many in the middle that things are getting worse, and that our capitalist sys-tem is escalating the disparity and inequality of wealth at an ever increasing speed – to warn them of their imminent slide into the lower class. The challenge for the Republican Party is to convince many in the middle that our capitalist system, despite the increas-ing inequality, provides everyone the opportunity to rise financial-ly into the upper class. The dificulty is that, as the disparity keeps increasing, the gulf between them and the wealthy appears to be more and more insurmountable.

Between 1979 and 2011, the true "middle class" (the 20% of households with income between the 40th and 60th percentile) saw their income rise by 24%. During that same time period, the top 1% saw their income rise 175% (7 times as fast). The US has one of the lowest minimum wages in the industiralized world, and the disparity is getting worse. In 1965, the average compensation for the CEOs of the 350 largest corporations in the US was 20 times their average worker's pay; by 1989, it was 58 times; and, by 2012, it had risen to 273 times. Is it any wonder that voters often vote in their own financial interest? Even when that vote is

otherwise ill-advised? Call it self-interest; call it financial survi-
val; call it protecting your family; or, call it greed. The name
doesn't matter as much as the fact that voters will often cast their
ballots for the candidate who appears to be more likely to support
measures that favor their economic class.

Chapter 8
Hero Worship

Unconsciously we all have a standard by which we measure other men, and if we examine closely we find that this standard is a very simple one, and is this: we admire them, we envy them, for great qualities we ourselves lack. Hero worship consists in just that. Our heroes are men who do things which we recognize, with regret, and sometimes with a secret shame, that we cannot do. We find not much in ourselves to admire, we are always privately wanting to be like somebody else. If everybody was satisfied with himself, there would be no heroes. — Mark Twain

As you get older it is harder to have heroes, but it is sort of necessary. — Ernest Hemingway

Be careful who you choose as your hero or who you choose to deify, be it Clay Aiken or Barack Obama. You put all you're hope and all your dreams and all your ideas about stuff into one human being. They're a human being they're going to let you down. — Craig Ferguson (Actor, Comedian)

Leadership consists of picking good men and helping them do their best. — Fleet Admiral Chester W Nimitz

Hero: the term is often used rather indiscriminately; but, there are those who tend to fall into the category for a great number of people. In the United States, the status of "hero" is often reserved for military leaders. This has a long pedigree in US history, and it is logical when one looks at how the United States came to exist.

The US began as a real-life *Survivor* episode. Farmers, millers and other "common people" came to America to establish colonies and settlements. They fought with the indigenous populations; they fought with each other; and, they fought surrogate battles for wars that were occurring between their sponsors back in Europe. A century and a half later, they organized into militia and armed forces to fight a revolution against England to gain their independence. And, the battles continued. Wars were almost commonplace as the new United States and the European nations struggled to determine who would command trade, commerce, and political control of much of the world. In such an environment, it would be logical for the successful military leaders to often be viewed as heroes to the common people.

In the epigraphs at the start of this chapter, Mark Twain found that heroes were people that we admire and envy for possessing traits that we lack. Although this may seem somewhat cynical, Twain was an inveterate cynic. Another writer, Ernest Hemingway, saw that heroes are harder and harder to acknowledge as we age, but that they are essentially necessary to have.

Perhaps the most balanced, although still somewhat cynical, view of heroes was the one offered (3rd epigraph) by the Scottish actor–write–comedian–personality–host–director–producer Craig Ferguson. Ferguson warned to "be careful who you choose as your hero" because they take on 'bigger than life' dimensions; and, since they are only human, "they're going to let you down." Perhaps they won't all let you down, but most of them do appear to do so.

Where many of them fail is in the requirement laid out by Fleet Admiral Chester Nimitz. Admiral Nimitz served as *Commander in Chief, Pacific Ocean Areas* for the US and its allies during World War II, and certainly knew good leadership when he saw it. He said (4th epigraph) that "leadership consists of picking good men and helping them do their best." Unfortunately, this is where many of the military leaders/heroes fail when they transition from the military to the political arena.

In the United States, prior military service is considered noble; candidates for office will advertise their past military roles openly to the public. It is often considered evidence of their loyalty, their civic pride, and their bravery. In many other countries, having a military background is often seen as suspicious. Many of these have seen former military leaders use their military connections to circumvent democratic institutions, and are therefore very wary of a politician who advertises and emphasizes his or her military background. In the US, this is quite the opposite — their military background is considered proof of their patriotism, loyalty, and leadership skills.

Consider what has happened with key leaders from virtually every war the United States has fought. Every individual on this list either served as President of the United States, or was a major party opposition candidate (Party follows name in parentheses).

War	Individual	Military Service
Revolution	George Washington (F)	General of the Army, Commander in Chief
	James Madison (D-R)	Orange County Militia Colonel
	James Monroe (D-R)	Army Major (wounded in battle); Virginia Militia Lieutenant Colonel
	Andrew Jackson (D)	Army enlisted (POW)
Northwest Terr. (Shawnee, Chippewa)	Wm Henry Harrison (W)	Army Captain (awarded for heroism by Major General "Mad" Anthony Wayne)
War of 1812	Andrew Jackson (D)	Army Major General
	Wm Henry Harrison (W)	Army Major General
	John Tyler (W)	Virginia Militia Captain
	Zachary Taylor (W)	Army Captain
	Winfield Scott (W)	Army Brigadier General
1st Seminole War	Andrew Jackson (D)	Army Major General
Black Hawk War	Zachary Taylor (W)	Army Colonel
	Abraham Lincoln (R)	Militia Captain
2nd Seminole War	Zachary Taylor (W)	Army Colonel
	Winfield Scott (W)	Army Brigadier General
Mexican-American	Zachary Taylor (W)	Army Brigadier General
	Franklin Pierce (D)	Army Brigadier General
	John Breckinridge (ND)	Kentucky Militia Major
	George McClellan (D)	Army Lieutenant
	Ulysses Grant (R)	Army Lieutenant
	Winfield Scott (W)	Army Major General
	Winfield Hancock (D)	Army Lieutenant
US Civil War	Ulysses Grant (R)	General of the Army
	George McClellan (D)	Army General-in-Chief
	Andrew Johnson (D)	Military Governor of Tennessee (rank: Brigadier General)
	Rutherford B Hayes (R)	Ohio Militia Major General
	James Garfield (R)	Army Major General
	Winfield Scott (W)	Army Major General
	Winfield Hancock (D)	Army Major General
	Chester Arthur (R)	Militia Quartermaster General

War	Individual	Military Service
Civil War *continued*	Benjamin Harrison (R)	Indiana Infantry Regiment Brigadier General
	James Weaver (P)	Army Colonel
	William McKinley (R)	Ohio Volunteers Brevet Major
Spanish-American	Theodore Roosevelt (R)	Cavalry Colonel
World War I	Harry Truman (D)	Field Artillery Major
	Dwight Eisenhower (R)	Army Captain
	Alf Landon (R)	Army Lieutenant
	Wendell Willkie (R)	Army Lieutenant
	Adlai Stevenson (D)	Navy Seaman
World War II	Dwight Eisenhower (R)	General of the Armies
	Strom Thurmond (SR)	Army Lieutenant Colonel
	John F Kennedy (D)	Navy Lieutenant (Purple Heart)
	Lyndon Johnson (D)	Navy Lieutenant Commander
	Barry Goldwater (R)	Air Force Reserve Major General
	Richard Nixon (R)	Navy Lieutenant Commander
	George Wallace (AI)	Air Corps Sergeant
	George McGovern (D)	Air Corps Lieutenant (awarded Distinguished Flying Cross)
	Gerald Ford (R)	Navy Lieutenant Commander
	Ronald Reagan (R)	Army Captain
	George HW Bush (R)	Navy Lieutenant JG (awarded Distinguished Flying Cross)
	Robert Dole (R)	Army Lieutenant (awarded two Purple Hearts and a Bronze Star for Valor)
Korea	Walter Mondale (D)	Army Corporal
	Ross Perot (I)	Navy Ensign
Viet Nam	George W Bush (R)	Air Force Reserve Lieutenant
	Al Gore (D)	Army Private
	John Kerry (D)	Navy Lieutenant (awarded three Purple Hearts, a Silver Star, and a Bronze Star for Valor)
	John McCain (R)	Navy Lieutenant Commander (POW; awarded Commendation Medal and Bronze Star)
(peace time service)	James K Polk (D)	Cavalry Captain
	Jimmy Carter (D)	Navy Lieutenant Commander

Of the 43 men who have served as President of the United States, over half of them (22; 51.2%) had prior military experience; and, every one of them was in a leadership, command position. In addition, a significant number of their opponents also held prior military experience, with most in a leadership, command position (only a few were in an enlisted position).

What does a leader do after a war ends? In the United States, you run for office! And, if the public generally perceives you as having been a "hero", you can probably count on a significant number of votes no matter what bone-head positions you espouse, and no matter how lousy a manager you are of people when you can't just order them to do what you want. And, there are a few examples of exemplary military officers who had no idea how to function in a political environment.

Example #14:

President Ulysses S Grant
(*born Hiram Ulysses Grant*)

Hiram Ulysses Grant (later, Ulysses S Grant) became the 18th President of the United States in the election of 1868. He was, to those states that were part of the Union, the hero of the Civil War. After a series of successes in the west, he was brought in to lead the Union forces against Confederate General Robert E Lee. This resulted in the Union victory over the Confederacy, and Lee's formal surrender in the McLean house in the village of Appomattox Court House, Virginia.

After the end of the war, President Johnson (who had assumed the office 6 days after the surrender, when Abraham Lincoln was assassinated) dispatched Grant to implement military control and reconstruction in the former Confederacy. Grant, however, implemented the radical reconstruction plan of Congress rather than the more conciliatory approach of the President. This frustrated the President, but endeared him to Congress.

In the election of 1868, Grant was unanimously nominated by the Republicans on the first ballot; Democrat, and former New York Governor, Horatio Seymour was a compromise candidate on the 23rd ballot in their convention. Grant never actively campaigned, and the election was surprisingly close considering the virtual reverence that Grant inspired (winning just 52.7% of the popular vote).

Following his inauguration, Grant proceded to: implement the Radical Reconstruction of the Republican congress; work to remove any residual elements of Confederate patriotism; completely eradicate any evidence of slavery; defeat and dismantle the Ku Klux Klan; and, protect the new citizenship status of African-Americans.

As a general, Grant is often assumed to have been a brilliant tactician; however, there are many who believe that his victory over the unquestionably brilliant Robert E Lee to have largely been the result of massive, brute force by a significantly larger army. Lee had been described by Army General-in-Chief Winfield Scott as "the very finest soldier I have ever seen", and had been offered command of the Union Army by Scott (he only declined after his home state of Virginia seceded).

As President, Grant showed a remarkable inability to distinguish between good people and bad for federal appointments. As a result, Grant was continually addressing Congressional investigations into charges of bribery of Cabinet Secretaries, federal corruption, and malfeasance.

His economic policies led to a debilitating deflation with a corresponding implementation of the gold standard. His foreign policies were more successful (avoiding war with Spain, resolving issues with Great Britain, and generally achieving international peace), although his policies led to the Great Sioux War (the war in which General Custer was killed). He also attempted to annex the Dominican Republic, but was blocked by Congress.

Economically, deflation led directly to a five year depression – with high unemployment, low prices, low profits, high bankruptcy filings, large trade deficits, and a run on the banks in the Panic of 1873 (known as the *Great Depression* until the downturn of the 1930s usurped the title). The greater problem was that Grant was reportedly, to put it kindly, a heavy drinker. That, combined with his poor choice of appointees and general non-involvement in many aspects of government, led to a series of damaging situations.

- Black Friday   1869: Grant had approved paper currency to pay government debt for Reconstruction. The intent was to buy it back in the future with gold. Jay Gould and James Fisk cornered the gold market by buying huge amounts. Abel Corbin (Grant's brother-in-law) helped them by convincing Grant not to act, and then letting Gould and Fisk know if he did decide to act. Rising gold prices caused stock prices to fall and gold to be at a premium; when Grant authorized the Treasury to sell off US Gold to alleviate the crisis, the price of gold fell rapidly. Assistant US Treasurer Daniel Butterfield (appointed by Grant on the recommendation of Corbin) notified Gould and Fisk in advance, and they got out without losing their accumulated gains. Most of the market investors lost fortunes, and the economy tanked for the next several years.

- NY Customs   1871: a corruption scandal at the New York Customs House arose under 2 Grant appointees (Moses Grinnell and Thomas Murphy), who set up a warehousing scheme at high prices to divert import duties to them. At the time, New York collected more import duties than any other port in the United States.

- Star Route   1872: postal delivery to remote, rural routes in the South and the Far West made postal delivery to these areas difficult and expensive. Mail to an address on one of these routes was marked on the package with an asterisk (hence the name, *Star Route*). Postmaster General Cresswell did not have the resources to deliver to all of these routes, so they were contracted out. Through bribery and fraudulent bidding, these routes went to contractors who overcharged for legitimate routes, and submitted bills for routes that did not even exist. A contractor in the Southwest (F P Sawyer) was found to have made over $500,000 a year through this scheme.

- Salaries   1873: On March 3rd, Grant signed an appropriations bill that raised his salary from $25,000 to $50,000, raised the salaries of Senators and Representatives from $5,000 to $7,500, and gave Congress a $5,000 bonus for the prior two years. Although the salary increases were legal, the retroactive bonuses were not; and, the law was passed in secret.

- Sanborn   1874: In 1872, Treasury Secretary George Bout-
                 well was elected to the Senate, and Grant ap-
                 pointed Assistant Secretary William Richardson
                 to replace him. Private contractors were often
                 hired to collect unpaid taxes, and John Sanborn
                 was contracted in this role. He was awarded
                 50% of whatever he collected after expenses, and
                 the Treasury Department pressured the IRS to
                 turn collections over to Sanborn (who collected
                 excessive commissions) to collect the taxes.

                 Sanborn collected $420,000 in taxes, and got to
                 keep $213,000 of it. He then split the profits
                 with his associates. Although Sanborn refused to
                 identify these "associates", it was widely believ-
                 ed to be Richardson and Senator Butler. While
                 the House was investigating, Richardson resign-
                 ed from his Cabinet post, and Grant appointed
                 him to the federal court in Massachusetts.

- Delano Affair 1875: Interior Secretary Columbus Delano was
                 discovered to have awarded fraudulent land
                 grants in return for bribes he was paid. He also
                 awarded lucrative mapping & surveying con-
                 tracts to John Delano (his son) and Orvil Grant
                 (the President's brother);   neither Delano nor
                 Grant ever did any work, and neither was even
                 qualified to do surveying.

                 After Delano resigned, his replacement fired all
                 of the top clerks in the Patent Office after discov-
                 ering that some were being paid without doing
                 any work, while others were being paid even
                 though they did not exist! He also had to fire
                 everyone in the Bureau of Indian Affairs for theft
                 and corruption.

- Pratt & Boyd   1875: US Attorney General George Williams
                 declined to proseute the commercial import firm
                 of Pratt & Boyd for fraudulent customhouse
                 reporting. The Senate investigation found that
                 Williams dropped the case after they had paid
                 $30,000 to Williams' wife.

- Whiskey Ring   1875: For years, whiskey distillers in the Mid-
                 West had evaded taxes by bribery, extortion, and
                 impressments. Regional Treasury Department
                 agents were complicit in the scheme, and the
                 monies realized (about $2,000,000 per year)

were split between the distillers and the agents. Altough there was no suggestion that Grant was personally involved, his poor judgment in appointees was again highlighted: appointees John McDonald (Internal Revenue Supervisor) and Orville Babcock (Grant's private secretary) were both indicted; Grant's other private secretary (Horace Porter) was also implicated, but never tried.

- Trading Post

1876: Brigadier General William Belknap, Secretary of War, was responsible for assigning private contracts to operate Trading Posts at forts where the Native Americans could trade or buy food, clothing, *etc*. These assignments were very financially rewarding, and the contract for the Trading Post at Fort Sill (Lawton, Oklahoma) was taken from the holder, and awarded to Caleb Marsh. Marsh was an old personal friend of Carrie Belknap (William's wife).

Marsh and Carrie Belknap allowed the prior contract holder (John Evans) to continue to run the Trading Post in return for $3,000 each quarter (*i.e.* extortion). Marsh and Belknap then split the money. Carrie died later that same year, but her husband and his 2nd wife continued to accept the extortion money for years. In 1876, it was discovered that they had accepted about $20,000 from this arrangement.

Belknap abruptly resigned. Although he was impeached by the House, he was not convicted by the Senate because by that time he was no longer a government employee.

- Cattelism

1876: Secretary of Navy George Robeson was provided $56,000,000 for construction projects for the Navy; but, $10,000,000 of that could never be found. Investigators assumed, but could not prove, that Robeson had embezzled it. In addition, it was established that Robeson had received hundreds of thousands of dollars in bribes to direct select Navy contracts to Alexander Cattell & Company.

Alexander Cattell was a former Republican US Senator from New Jersey, and Secretary Robeson had been a Civil War General under Grant (who appointed him). Although the Senate investigation was strongly negative, Grant never fired him, and Robeson never resigned.

- Safe Burglary 1876: Private Secretary Orville Babcock was indicted for being complicit in a very complicated scheme to derail an investigation and get a Grant critic convicted for something he didn't do.

  Corrupt contractors in Washington DC were being tried for graft. Fake Secret Service agents planted phony evidence in the prosecuting District Attorney's safe. Fellow conspirators then broke in, blew open the safe, stole the fake evidence, and brought it to the house of Columbus Alexander (the reformer & Grant critic). The fake agents arrested the burglars, who then were freed when they perjured themselves and said that Alexander was the ring leader.

  Alexander was acquitted after two of the "burglars" turned state's evidence, and Babcok was indicted as the chief conspirator in the plot. He was acquitted as a result of what was almost certainly jury tampering.

All of the evidence (and the consensus of his biographers) was that President Grant was personally an honest man. His problem was that he was also a fairly simple man. Give him a cigar and some liquor, and he was content. As a graduate of West Point, he was educated in cavalry, infantry, artillery, military strategy and tactics, mathematics and French; he was, by nature, suspicious of highly intelligent people. And, he had neither the intelligence nor the education to personally comprehend the intricacies of an economy as complex as that of the United States. As a result of all this, he tended to rely on relatives, old friends, and friends he had made during his command in the Civil War. And, according to his son, Grant was "incapable of supposing his friends to be dishonest." And, once a friend of Grant, always a friend of Grant: his Attorney General, George Williams, said that once Grant formed a friendship, it "took hold with hooks of steel".

A pefect example of this was his Private Secretary, Orville Babcock. Babcock was involved in the Black Friday scheme to corner the gold market; he was knee deep in the Whiskey Ring tax evasion enterprise; and, he was apparently the leader of the Safe Burglary plot. How did Grant respond? He appointed him Chief Lighthouse Inspector, a well paid federal job that demanded very little from the incumbent and might easily be corrupted (at that time, the US was busy building lighthouses along the east coast to facilitate safer shipping). Fortunately for the country, Babcock never had the opportunity to abuse yet another position, as he drowned a few years later (at the age of 48) in Ponce Inlet, Florida when the ferry that was bringing him ashore overturned in a storm.

President Grant's penchant for appointing friends, relatives, and former military comrades was well known even when he was still in his 1st term — it didn't stop the people from re-electing their "hero". In the leadup to the 1872 election, Senator Charles Sumner openly accused Grant of gross nepotism; although the electorate seemed not to care, this was not an exaggeration.

- The US Minister to Guatemala was Silas Hudson (his cousin);

- the Consul to Leipzig (Germany) was Reverend M J Cramer (his brother-in-law – sister Mary's husband);

- the New Orleans Collector of Customs was James Casey (another brother-in-law – married to Emma, his wife's sister), who stole fees to supplement his income;

- a White House usher, who made side money by selling supposedly "inside information" to tourists was Frederick Dent (yet another brother-in-law – wife's brother);

- many of the Cabinet positions and other plum government appointments went to former military comrades; and,

- it has been calculated that more than 40 Grant relatives were given positions where they drew federal salaries while Grant was President.

Presient Ulysses S Grant was not a crook. He was an American hero to much of the country. He was also naïve, gullible, and loyal to a fault. His choice in appointees was perhaps the worst of any President in US history; and, the public was aware, or at least had been told, of this even prior to his re-election run. But, as a hero, that was conveniently overlooked by the voters.

Example #15:

President Zachary Taylor

Zachary Taylor was effectively the "anti-politician" elected President. Taylor had spent his entire adult life in the military:

- taking command of Fort Knox (Indiana) in 1811 (Captain);
- defending Fort Harrison (Indiana), and defeating Tecumseh in the War of 1812 (Major);
- commanding Fort Howard (Wisconsin) for 2 years (Major);
- commanding Fort Robertson (Louisiana) – buying a plantation, and moving his family there (Lieutenant Colonel);
- commanding Fort Snelling and Fort Crawford (both Minnesota), and fighting Black Hawk in the 'Black Hawk War' (Colonel);
- fighting and winning the Christmas Day Battle of Lake Okeechobee in the 2nd Seminole War (Brigadier General);
- commanding all US troops in Florida for 2 years, and then all US troops in the southern half of the US west of the Mississippi for the next 3 years (Brigadier General); and,
- deployed along the Rio Grande River at the start of the Mexican-American War, he won decisive victories over much larger forces at Palo Alto and Resaca de la Palma. Monterrey was considered impregnable, but Taylor inflicted heavy losses on the Mexican forces, captured the city in 3 days, and forced the Mexican Army to retreat. After most of his forces were sent to assist General Scott at Veracruz, the remnant of his forces were attacked by Mexican General Antonio López de Santa Anna at the Battle of Buena Vista. Taylor lost 700 of his 6,000 troops, but inflicted more than twice that loss on Santa Anna, who fled in retreat.

Taylor became a national hero for having consistently, throughout his military career, overcome superior enemy forces to achieve victory. Although he had never been political (he had never even voted) he was nominated by the Whig Party as their Presidential candidate in the 1848 election. This was rather odd, as he had never revealed any personal views on the political issues of the day, and he was a plantation owner with more than 200 slaves (the Whigs opposed slavery).

In 1835, his daughter (Sarah) married a young lieutenant in his command, but died three months later of malaria. That made the lieutenant Taylor's son-in-law. That son-in-law was Jefferson Davis, the future President of the Confederacy.

In the election, Taylor never spelled out his political views, virtually never campaigned (leaving that to his running mate, Millard Fillmore), and only insisted that he wanted to ease the regional tensions that had been building over the issue of slavery. His only real priority appeared to be the preservation of the Union — he was staunchly opposed to secession.

The leaders of the Whig Party convinced him to head their ticket despite his obvious lack of interest in politics, his reluctance, his vague beliefs, and his ownership of slaves. His hero status stood him in good stead, however, and he and Fillmore won the three-way election outright, defeating Democrat Lewis Cass and Free Soil Party candidate (and former President) Martin Van Buren.

Once he was inaugurated, it became clear that his vague lack of views was not simply a reluctance to reveal them — he apparently didn't have any. Despite owning slaves himself, he did not support the spread of slavery into the territories newly acquired from Mexico; however, he also did not push to restrict or eliminate slavery. In fact, to avoid having to take a position, he encouraged California and New Mexico to skip the "territorial stage", draft constitutions, and apply for admission to statehood. That way, they could decide the status of slavery, and he would not have to get involved.

Taylor saw the role of President as an executor, not an implementer. As a result, he felt that the President should never veto anything passed by Congress unless it violated the Constitution. He felt that Congress should be negotiating and making the decisions. Taylor kept his distance from Congress and let Senate Majority Leader Henry Clay make most of the decisions. Clay ultimately pushed through the Compromise of 1850, which allowed statehood for California (without slavery), while keeping the other territories under federal control. There were other features of the Compromise Act (banning the slave trade, keeping slavery in Washington DC, requiring northern states to return runaway southern slaves, *etc.*). It was an excellent example of a compromise: nobody from either side liked it! This bill, however, never reached Taylor's desk; he died before it got that far. So, although we can assume that he would have signed it (considering his views on presidential vetoes), we don't know his thoughts on it.

Taylor went so far as to assign his Cabinet posts on the basis of regional distribution. His Cabinet Secretaries were all Whigs, but they came from the north, the south, and the west on a proportional basis. Taylor had no experience nor skill in debate, negotiation, compromise, or diplomacy. His presidency, short though it was, was essentially a precursor to a line uttered by Los Angeles taxi driver Rodney King during the Los Angeles riots in 1992: "Can we all get along?"

Taylor wanted the regional tensions to simply go away, but his lack of diplomatic skills did nothing to bring that about. In addition, he was plagued by a "scandal" that was not of his doing, but which a more reasoned approach to appointing Cabinet offices might have avoided.

His Secretary of War, George Crawford, had been the Governor of Georgia, and represented the heirs of George Galphin in a suit against the government for interest payments on a debt which the federal government had paid (but not paid interest). It was finally settled while Crawford was Secretary of War. The settlement, in Galphin's favor, awarded nearly $200,000 in interest. Under the original legal agreement, Crawford got to keep half of it.

Although Congress was in session, Crawford did not bring the issue to their attention. Instead, he approached Attorney General Reverdy Johnson and Treasury Secretary William Meredith. They approved the interest payment and signed off on it. Crawford received over $94,000 from the settlement, and Meredith kept $3,000 for himself for 'facilitating' the payment.

When news of the settlement became common knowledge, the public was outraged. Crawford resigned from the Cabinet, and lived the rest of his life off the money he had received. Neither Johnson nor Meredith suffered any consequences.

President Taylor died in early July of 1850 after only 16 months in office. He reportedly died of extreme gastrointestinal problems probably caused by Washington's open sewers and poor sanitation at the time (several members of the Cabinet suffered from similar compaints).

Like Grant, Taylor was personally honest. His problem, however, was different than Grant's. He was, to put it mildly, extremely politically naïve. He appointed people on the basis of where they came from regionally (so long as they were Whigs), and never considered what "baggage" they might bring with them to the job. He avoided interaction with Congress so that they could 'do their job' without his interference at a time when Presidential leadership could have potentially had tremendous impact — especially considering that the President was a slave holder from a party that officially opposed slavery.

Zachary Taylor was not a "bad" President; he was simply a thoroughly ineffective one. Fortunately, nothing of any great import was occurring internationally, as he completely deferred all international decisions to his Secretary of State (the former Senator from Delaware), who had even less foreign and diplomatic experience than Taylor.

We have no way of knowing how Taylor's administration would have evolved over the full four-year term, as Taylor died only 16 months (492 days) into his term (giving him one of the shortest presidential terms in US history — longer than only William Henry Harrison's 31 days, and James Garfield's 199 days). There can be no question, however, as to *why* he was elected: he had no political history, skills, or interest; he had no diplomatic skills; he had no administrative skills outside a military environment; he didn't campaign for the office; and, he apparently had no strong views about anything. None of this mattered to the electorate in 1848, for he had one very important thing going for him: he was a hero, a war hero.

Chapter 9
Tunnel Vision

It's that one thing that you're passionate about, that you end up developing tunnel vision for and everything else tends to fall by the wayside. — Johnny Galecki (actor)

To be a tennis champion, you have to be inflexible. You have to be stubborn. You have to be arrogant. You have to be selfish and self-absorbed. Kind of tunnel vision almost.
— Chris Evert (tennis champion)

Tunnel Vision is actually a medical condition (sometimes known as "Kalnienk Vision") which has been defined as a loss of peripheral vision with a simultaneous retention of central vision that results in a limited, circular, 'tunnel-like' field of vision. It can have a wide variety of causes, such as glaucoma, hallucinogenic drug use, or a migraine headache (during the aura phase). For our purposes, however, we are more concerned with the figurative meaning of the term rather than the medical. In that sense, *tunnel vision* generally refers to a highly focused, very limited perspective.

This figurative sense is what actor Johnny Galecki (best known for his role as Dr. Leonard Hofstadter on *The Big Bang Theory*) was referencing when he said (top epigraph) that you can end up developing "tunnel vision" for whatever it is "that you're passionate about". This is also the sense in which Chris Evert was using the term in referring to the focus, the obsession, and the lack of all peripheral distractions that are the hallmark of a champion.

This same obsessive focus, this loss of peripheral distractions, also shows up in voters. One issue can become so central, so important, to a voter that other issues have little to no bearing on their electoral decision making at all. This is actually so common that there is a term used specifically to refer to it: *single-issue politics* (where this "single issue" is often called the *defining issue*).

Generally, when political parites form around a single issue, they have very limited (if any) success. Nevertheless, there are examples of single-issue, "tunnel vision parties" from all over the world. Consider a few of those defining issues that have come to so dominate a political election or campaign that they generated a "single issue party":

- the *Bloc Québécois* (Canada) formed to pursue a separation of Québec from Canada;

- the *Scottish National Party* (Scotland) formed originally to promote the dissolution of the United Kingdom;

- *Partij voor de Dieren* (Netherlands) has animal rights as its sole focus, as has the *Animal Justice Party* (Australia);

- the *Australian Sex Party* formed to counter the growing influence of religion in politics;

- the *US Marijuana Party* (United States) wants the federal legalization of marijuana;

- the *Right to Life Party* (United States) was founded in 1970 for the purpose of blocking abortion from becoming legal in New York;

- the *Pacifist Party* (United States) is an anti-nuclear, anti-war party;

- the *Lavender Party* (France) supports full rights for the LGBT community; and,

- the *Prohibition Party* (United States) formed in 1869 with the intent of making alcoholic beverages illegal.

Much more common than an entire political party dedicated to a single issue is the individual voter so focused on a single issue that other positions virtually become non-issues. So, in addition to organized political parties (which, as said, are often small and ineffective), what are these specific issues that a voter may consider to be the "defining issue" for their decision as to which candidate to support, regardless of any other positions they may espouse? Examples would include:

- the Right to Life
- the Right to Choose;
- Prayer in Schools;
- the Right to Bear Arms;
- the legalization of "soft drugs";
- the Minimum Wage;
- the rights of Unions;
- Equitable Taxation;
- LGBT Rights;
- Freedom of Religion;
- Universal Health Care;
- Affirmative Action;
- Gambling / Casinos;
- Public Education;
- Fracking;
- Environmentalism;
- Climate Change;
- Immigration;

  and on, and on, and on, …

There is almost no end to the issues that some voters consider so important that it overshadows anything else a candidate says or does. In local elections, the issue may even be so trivial as to seem ludicrous to someone from outside that electoral district (for example, the handling of on-street parking in the 'downtown area', or a traffic light at the "corner of Main Street").

Unfortunately, this focus on a single issue often results in some very poor choices being made by the electorate. Consider a few examples. The first two are historical from the 19th century, and revolve around the issue of slavery. The final example is modern, and appears to be focused almost exclusively on immigration.

Example #16:

US Representative Preston Brooks

Representative Preston Smith Brooks (1819–1857) was elected as the Democratic Representative for South Carolina's 4th Congressional District in 1852, and was twice re-elected (serving until his death in 1857).

In 1820, during the administration of James Monroe, Congress had passed the *Missouri Compromise*. This compromise, developed by Speaker of the House Henry Clay, outlawed slavery in all of the Louisiana Purchase north of a particular latitude with the exception of the future state of Missouri (hence the name "Missouri Compromise").

In 1854, however, Democratic Senators Stephen Douglas (Illinois) and Andrew Butler (South Carolina) proposed what became known as the *Kansas-Nebraska Act*. This opened up thousands of acres for settlers and made a future transcontinental railroad more feasible, but also gave these new settlers the right to decide for themselves whether the new areas would be pro- or anti-slavery — effectively repealing the Missouri Compromise in these areas. The result was disastrous, as settlers of both positions flooded into the new area, leading to an armed conflict that would become known as *Bleeding Kansas*.

In 1856, the Senate was embroiled in this Bleeding Kansas crisis, and Senator Charles Sumner (R-Massachusetts) delivered a long speech (May 19th and 20th) that sharply criticized the Kansas-Nebraska Act as the cause of the strife, and personally blamed Senator Butler for it. In his speech, Sumner was directly referencing Butler when he said:

> "The senator from South Carolina has read many books of chivalry, and believes himself a chivalrous knight with sentiments of honor and courage. Of course, he has chosen a mistress to whom he has made his vows, and who, though ugly to others, is always lovely to him; though polluted in the sight of the world, is chaste in his sight — I mean the harlot, slavery."

Two days later, on May 22nd, Butler's cousin (Preston Brooks) attacked him in the Senate chamber. Sumner was seated at his desk writing a letter when Representative Brooks confronted him, accusing him of libeling the state of South Carolina and Senator Butler. When Sumner began to stand up, Brooks repeatedly hit Senator Sumner over the head with his walking cane. The cane was constructed of *gutta-percha*, a Malaysian wood that is rich in natural latex, is extremely strong, and has a certain flexibility that enables it to resist shattering on impact; it was very popular in the latter half of the 19th century for furniture and other uses where strength was paramount. It was topped by a gold cap, which made the cane a deadly weapon, and Senator Sumner was nearly killed — suffering serious injuries from the attack.

Sumner collapsed to the floor, where Brooks continued to beat him with the cane. With blood streaming from his head wounds, making it impossible for him to see, Sumner staggered up the aisle and collapsed unconscious. Brooks only stopped when his cane finally broke apart. Brooks then calmly walked out of the Senate, while Sumner was carried out to a doctor.

Sumner, suffering from headaches, nightmares, traumatic brain injury, and what we now call PTSD, was unable to remain in the Senate. Rather than replace him, however, the Massachusetts legislature decided to reappoint him and keep his seat empty until he was able to resume his office — as a reminder of what had happened. From that point forward, both Senators and Representatives would arm themselves before entering the House or Senate chamber. Sumner required a long convalescence, but did return to the Senate in 1859. He suffered from chronic pain and debilitation until he died in 1874.

Over a million copies of Sumner's speech were distributed in the north, and northern papers praised Sumner and were outraged at the South for its "barbarism", while in the South, hundreds of new canes were sent to Brooks by supporters from all over the south.

Sumner was a slight, scholarly, 45 year old; Brooks was a 36 year old who had been expelled from South Carolina College (today, the University of South Carolina) for threatening police officers with a gun, had fought as a Colonel in the Palmetto Regiment in the Mexican-American War (less than 30% of whom returned alive), and used the walking cane because of a hip injury suffered in a duel over which candidate to support for South Carolina Governor. It was not a "fair fight" by any means.

Brooks was tried in a DC criminal court, and convicted of assault; he was fined $300. A House attempt to oust him from Congress failed; but, on July 15th, he resigned his seat. The people of South Carolina, however, re-elected him in a special election held August 1st. They then re-elected him in the general election in November.

The *Richmond Enquirer* editorialized that "we consider the act good in conception, better in execution, and best of all in consequences." Other southern papers joined in their adulation of Brooks for the attack. When Brooks returned to South Carolina after having resigned, over ten thousand supporters rallied to greet him. Special trains had to be scheduled to bring in all of the people who wanted to see him.

Representative Preston Brooks is an excellent example of tunnel vision. The people of his Congressional District in South Carolina (and, in fact, from virtually all corners of the south) were so focused on the issue of slavery that nothing else seemed to matter.

- Was he a bully? No, they argued, for he was simply defending the honor of his cousin and his region.

- Wasn't he convicted of assault? Yes, but by a court in Washington, DC.

- Did he act in a manner consistent with what was expected of a member of Congress? Yes, because chivalry only applied to gentlemen, and Brooks maintained that Sumner's speech clearly marked him as a drunken, low-life, scoundrel not deserving of chivalry (in fact, Sumner was a religious, well-traveled, Harvard-educated, non-drinker).

But, Preston Brooks did not act alone. If he had been by himself, other Senators would have intervened and stopped the assault. He had friends who had gone to the Senate with him to witness and, if necessary, participate in the attack.

Representative Laurance Keitt (D- South Carolina) protected Brooks during the attack from those who would have separated the two — we'll look at him next. In addition, Representative Henry Edmundson (D-Virginia) was also there to ensure that nobody intervened to stop the attack. Edmundson, who would serve seven terms in Congress, had been arrested back in 1854 during the initial debates over passage of the Kansas-Nebraska Act. The Whig Congressman from Ohio's 3rd District, Lewis Campbell, was getting the House stirred up with his rhetoric, and Edmundson went to attack him. He was restrained by other members of the House, and he was then arrested by the Sergeant-at-Arms. Both came to the Senate that day in 1856 to support and protect Preston

Brooks during his attack on Sumner. The 4th member of the attack team was Mississippi Congressman William Barksdale (below).

Example #17:

US Representative Laurence Keitt

Laurence Massillon Keitt (1824–1864) was elected to Congress as the Representative for South Carolina's 3rd District, and served for more than seven years, from 1853 to 1860.

Representative Keitt holds the unique, though not enviable, record of being the only US elected official to be directly involved in two separate acts of violence in the federal legislative chambers. He supported Preston Brooks in his attack on Senator Charles Sumner in 1856 (above), and he instigated an attack on another Congressman two years later in the House chamber.

In 1856, when Congressman Brooks went to the Senate chamber to attack Sumner, Representative Keitt went along (with Mississippi Rep. William Barksdale, and Virginia Congressman Henry Edmundson) to make sure that nobody separated them. After Brooks began the attack on Sumner, Representative Ambrose Murray (R-New York), Senator John Crittenden (A-Kentucky; the oldest member of the Senate), and several others tried to restrain Brooks before he killed Sumner. Keitt pulled a pistol from his waistband, pointed it at them, and shouted "Let them be!" The House voted to censure Keitt for his role in the affair, and he, like Brooks, resigned in protest. But, also like Brooks, the voters of South Carolina returned him to office less than a month later in the special election called to fill the newly vacant seat.

Two years later, Representative Keitt was again involved in a Congressional brawl when he took offense with Pennsylvania Congressman Galusha Grow (R-Pennsylvania). Representative Grow, who would later become the Speaker of the House, had earlier been a Democrat (converting after the Kansas-Nebraska Act was passed). During a heated debate in the House on February 5, 1858, Representative Grow crossed over from the "Republican side" of the chamber to the "Democratic side) to talk with another Congressman. Keitt took offense and derisively told Grow to go back and sit down, and referred to him as a "black Republican puppy". Grow did not take this well, and told Keitt that "no negro-driver shall crack his whip over me". Keit leaped at him, attacked him, and shouted that he would choke him to death for that comment.

In what a sports announcer might call a "bench clearing brawl", about 50 Congressmen joined the fray. It was a knock-down, brutal, floor fight until Congressman Cadwallader Washburn (R-Wisconsin) threw a punch that only glanced off of Representative William Barksdale (D-Mississippi). Washburn, who would later found General Mills, had not landed a solid punch, but had knocked Barksdale's wig loose. Barksdale, understandably embarrassed, quickly put the wig back on — only, in the confusion, he put it on backwards. Both sides got laughing so hard at Barksdale's appearance that the fight just evaporated.

Keitt once explained the South's position on slavery during a speech to the assembled House of Representatives on January 25, 1860. In it, he said that "The anti-slavery party contends that slavery is wrong in itself, and the Government is a consolidated national democracy. We of the South contend that slavery is right, and that this is a confederate Republic of sovereign States." That voiced, in a nutshell, what led to the US Civil War.

Keitt was again re-elected by the voters of South Carolina. Keitt was an outspoken member of the Congressional group known as the *Fire Easters* — a caucus of radical southerners who resisted any effort to compromise or find common ground on the slavery issue, and who steadfastly demanded southern secession from the United States. When South Carolina officially seceded (December 20, 1860), Keitt resigned from Congress. Six weeks later (February 8, 1861), South Carolina joined the new Confederate States of America. Keitt served as a South Carolina delegate to the Provisional Confederate Congress, and then as a Colonel in the CSA Army. Keitt was fatally wounded in the Battle of Cold Harbor (June 1, 1864), and died the next day.

Although, as with Representative Preston Brooks, the voters of South Carolina repeatedly returned him to office despite having been censured, participated in the near murder of Senator Sumner, and having initiated a physical brawl on the floor of the House of Representatives. Clearly, their focus was only on the slavery issue, and that tunnel vision kept "fire eater" Keitt in Congress.

Not all voters were so narrowly focused, though: former South Carolina Attorney General James Petigru opposed both secession and the Confederacy, and famously said that "South Carolina is too small for a republic, and too large for an insane asylum."

Example #18:

Arizona Sheriff Paul Babeu

Paul Raymond Babeu (b. 1969) first ran for the position of Sheriff of Pinal County (Arizona) in 2008. He challenged the incumbent, Democrat Christopher Vásquez. Winning by a healthy margin (54% to 46%), Babeu became the first Republican to be elected Sheriff in the 133 year history of Pinal County.

The following year, Babeu reorganized the Department, and replaced the entire command leadership team. Initially, he appears to have been an effective Sheriff: emergency response times dropped by 40%; significant grants were awarded to fund Department activities; he removed speed cameras as promised in the campaign; and, he implemented tough employee standards.

He was also accepted by his peers both in Arizona and the nation, being selected President of the Arizona Sheriffs' Association, and being named National Sheriff of the Year in 2011. Sheriff Babeu, however, is an outspoken critic of the federal government when it comes to the issue of illegal immigration. He maintains that Pinal County, which includes most of the area between Phoenix and Tucson, is a major corridor for illegal drug and human smuggling. He was even brought in by Arizona Senators John McCain (R-AZ) and Jon Kyl (R-AZ) to aid in drafting their proposed *Border Security Plan*.

The youngest sheriff in Arizona; recognition from both of the state's Senators; National Sheriff of the Year; President of the Arizona Sheriffs' Association: Sheriff Babeu must have thought that there were great things in his future. In fact, in late October 2011, Babeu formally announced the formation of an exploratory committee for a run for the US Congress. Arizona had redrawn its Congressional Districts following the 2010 census, and Babeu was exploring a run for the newly redrawn 4th Congressional District.

The 4th District was drawn such that it is heavily Republican, and a win in the Republican primary would virtually assure a win in the general election. The one-term incumbent in the 1st District, Paul Gosar, had been endorsed in 2010 by Babeu; but, after the Districts were redrawn for the 2012 election, Gosar ended up competing in the 4th rather than the 1st. That put him in the Republican primary with Babeu. Pinal County, where Babeu was the popular sheriff, was divided and put into 4 different Congressional districts. Nevertheless, it appeared that Gosar would have his hands full with Babeu.

In February 2012, however, José Orozco came forward with claims about Babeu. He claimed that he and Babeu had met in an online dating site, and that they had been lovers for the prior 6 years. If that wasn't bad enough for Babeu (running against a moralistic Tea Party favorite in Gosar), Orozco also let it be known that Babeu was aware that he was an undocumented alien. That ran counter to Babeu's fierce anti-immigrant stand as Sheriff. He also claimed that Babeu had threatened him with deportation if he didn't keep his mouth shut, and that he had e-Mails and text messages between the two of them that would substantiate everything he said.

Babeu denied most of what Orozco claimed, but did publicly acknowledge that he was gay on February 18th. His spokesman said this would not affect his run for Congress; however, Babeu did resign as co-chair of Mitt Romney's Arizona campaign. Three months later (on May 11, 2012), Babeu announced he was withdrawing from the House race, and would instead run for re-election as Sheriff of Pinal County. He was re-elected with 54% of the vote (to 33% for the Democrat, and 13% for an Independent candidate). The Pinal County election was a complete rout by the Republican Party – capturing nearly every elected office, and sweeping almost all of the incumbent Democrats out of office.

At the end of August (August 31st), 2 months prior to the election, the Arizona Solicitor General exonerated Babeu of any criminal violations, and announced that José Orozco was guilty – at most – of a misdemeanor, and would not be prosecuted. It is interesting to note that the Solicitor General in Arizona is appointed by, and reports to, the State Attorney General. In Babeu's case, Attorney General Tom Horne recused himself from the Babeu investigation as he was a well known Republican activist, that he and Babeu had supported each other politically for many years and had a close personal relationship. Instead, he appointed Solicitor General David Cole to run the investigation. Cole, who had been appointed Solicitor General a year earlier by Horne, was charged with determining if there was sufficient evidence to charge his boss' friend, Sheriff Babeu, with abuse of power (by threatening Orozco with deportation). Surpise, surprise: he decided there wasn't.

It really isn't critical for this review to know whether Sheriff Babeu was guilty of threatening Orozco with deportation or not. What is more interesting is the apparent lack of interest that the electorate had with regard to his obvious hypocrisy. Babeu was the darling of the very conservative Republican base in his county, and they have "tunnel vision" when it comes to the issue of illegal immigration and undocumented workers. Babeu was outspokenly opposed to this, and struck a very high moral tone when it came to conservative social issues. The evidence, however, was far less conservative. He acknowledged being gay and having a sexual relationship with Orozco (an illegal, undocumented worker); he only denied that he had ever used his position to threaten Orozco with deportation when the relationship went sour.

There is no question that Sheriff Babeu is one tough SOB. He served 20 years in the National Guard (first in Massachusetts, his home state, and then in Arizona, his adopted state). He spent a year and a half commanding 700 soldiers in support of the US Border Patrol, served a tour in Iraq, and graduated from the Arizona Law Enforcement Academy ranked 1st in his graduating class as the top police recruit in the state.

In 2012, Babeu informed the Pinal County supervisors that he had acquired a lot of equipment under the federal *1033 Program* (the program under which the Defense Logistics Agency distributes excess military equipment to local and state police agencies). Babeu informed the supervisors that the sale of this equipment should realize between a quarter and a half million dollars for the County, and would help balance his Department's $47 million budget. The *Arizona Republic* newspaper ran an exposé on August 20, 2014 on the sale (which was a violation of the 1033 Program), and the Defense Logistics Agency ordered Babeu to get back any "equipment his office distributed to non-police organizations".

In the final analysis, he may be a good sheriff by most standards, but he is morally hypocritical and obviously not as squeaky clean as he presents himself. Nonetheless, the voters exhibited tremendous tunnel vision regarding his anti-immigration position, and re-elected him with almost exactly the same percentage of the vote as he had received 4 years earlier (before any of this was known).

Chapter 10
Manipulation

The Iraq War was the biggest issue for people of my genera-tion in the West. It was also the clearest case, in my living memory, of media manipulation and the creation of a war through ignorance.   — Julian Assange (WikLeaks founder)

Madison Avenue is a very powerful aggression against private consciousness: a demand that you yield your private con-sciousness to public manipulation.
— Marshall McLuhan (sociologist)

Manipulation is defined as a "skillful handling, controlling, or using something or someone." That would apply to a very wide range of activities — from sculpture and art to working with tools to convincing a friend as to where to eat. But, in the case of politics, it is specifically *psychological manipulation* that is of interest.

Psychological manipulation is the use of social influence to alter the behavior or perceptions of others, often through some rather questionable means. In the case of politics, there are four common means often used in an attempt to change the perception of the electorate to alter their voting behavior (*i.e.* to *psychologically manipulate* them). These are:

- Mislead   to deliberately give someone the wrong idea about something

- Misquote   to deliberately or accidentally report a quote inaccurately

- Misdirect   to knowingly send someone off in the wrong direction

- Misrepresent   to give a false and misleading account of something

Mislead   The classic example of misleading someone is to give them a non-choice by offering a non-comprehensive set of alternatives. "Have you stopped beating your dog?" There is no acceptable way to answer this: "Yes, I have stopped." (which implies that you <u>were</u> beating your dog), or "No, I have not" (which implies that you are <u>still</u> beating your dog). The proper answer is more likely "That question is null, as I have never beaten my dog." To someone listening to the conversation, however, the "easy" answers (yes and no) are clearly misleading, and will certainly give the listener the wrong impression.

As simple as this appears to be, this approach is often used in an only slightly more refined format in the field of politics "President Nixon, are you going to continue to have the Air Force bombing targets in Cambodia to disrupt the flow of supplies to the Viet Cong?" There would have been a tremendous desire to show the media that the US was taking a prudent approach to the war by trying to stop the resupply of Viet Cong guerillas operating in South Viet Nam; but, either a yes or no would also be an implied admission that the US had expanded the war to a neutral nation.

Misquote   Tyically, a misquote is an attempt either to get the listener to believe that a respected source has said something they never actually said, or to get a damaging admission attributed to someone who never said it. An excellent example of this first type of misquote was that put forward by the *Heartland Institute* in April 2014.

The Heartland Institute is a conservative/libertarian think tank headquartered in Chicago. It was founded in 1984 by David Padden, a founding director of the *Cato Institute* in Washington, DC (another conservative/libertarian think tank). The Cato Institute was originally founded back in 1974 as the *Charles Koch Foundation* (we'll hear more about the Koch brothers in Chapter 13); and, it appears that much of the funding for the Heartland Institute is coming from the same sources. They posted a meme to Facebook® that showed a photo of the late comedian George Carlin along with a quote attributed to him. The problem is that Carlin never said it.

There are numerous George Carlin websites on the internet run by fans, critics, and even his daughter (Kelly). There is a "bogus Carlin Quote List" on GeorgeCarlin.net that provides a fairly extensive listing of things credited to Carlin that he apparently never actually said (at least nobody can find it anywhere in the thousands of hours of tapes of his shows, appearances and talks).

Snopes.com® (the best of the internet "authenticity checkers") has also weighed in on why a list of this sort is even necessary. Barbara and David Mikkelson (the founders and operators of Snopes.com) wrote that "just about any unsourced list of witty observations about politics and social mores will eventually become credited to humorist George Carlin as it passes from inbox to inbox". An example would be the quote usually labeled as "The Paradox of our Time". Attributed to Carlin even before his death in 2008 (while he could still deny he ever said it), Carlin commented on this specific quote in 2001. At that time, he called this particular meme "a sappy load of shit".

The meme posted by the Heartland Institute, which does not appear to have been created by them but which they reposted to Facebook with apparently no attempt to verify its accuracy, is shown below.

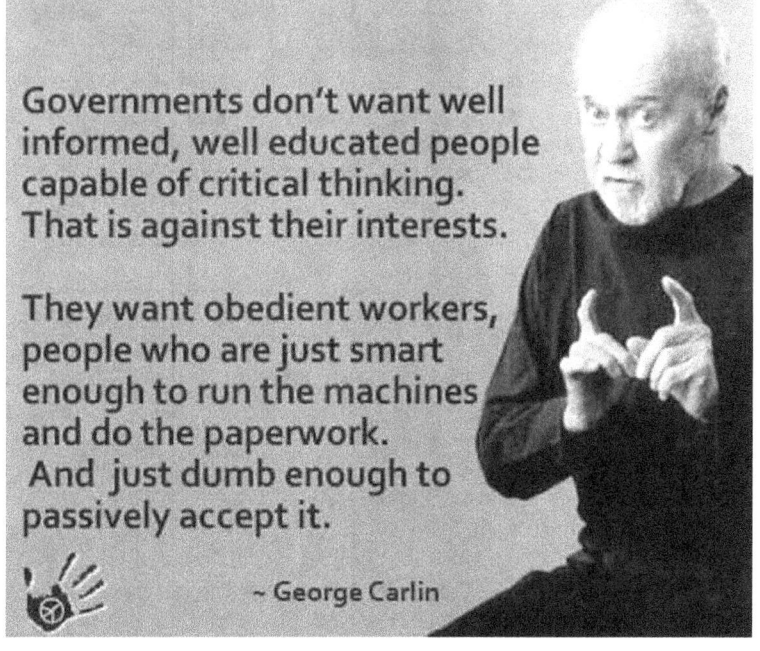

As stated, the problem with this quote is that it is a blatant misquote of something that Carlin said on stage in December 2005. A video clip of that performance was posted by Kelly Carlin-McCall (George's daughter, and only child) along with a request to help her correct the bastardized version floating on the internet.

A transcript of what George actually said is as follows.

> The real owners are the big wealthy business interests that control things and make all the important decisions. Forget the politicians, they're an irrelevancy. The politicians are put there to give you the idea that you have freedom of choice. You don't. You have no choice. You have owners. They own you. They own everything. They own all the important land. They own and control the corporations. They've long since bought and paid for the Senate, the Congress, the statehouses, the city halls. They've got the judges in their back pockets. And they own all the big media companies, so that they control just about all of the news and information you hear. They've got you by the balls. They spend billions of dollars every year lobbying, lobbying to get what they want. Well, we know what they want; they want more for themselves and less for everybody else.

> But I'll tell you what they don't want. They don't want a population of citizens capable of critical thinking. **They don't want well-informed, well-educated people capable of critical thinking. They're not interested in that.** That doesn't help them. That's against their interests. They don't want people who are smart enough to sit around the kitchen table and figure out how badly they're getting fucked by a system that threw them overboard 30 fucking years ago.

> **You know what they want? Obedient workers people who are just smart enough to run the machines and do the paperwork but just dumb enough to passively accept** all these increasingly shittier jobs with the lower pay, the longer hours, reduced benefits, the end of overtime and the vanishing pension that disappears the minute you go to collect it. And, now, they're coming for your Social Security. They want your fucking retirement money. They want it back, so they can give it to their criminal friends on Wall Street. And you know something? They'll get it. They'll get it all, sooner or later, because they own this fucking place. It's a big club, and you ain't in it. You and I are not in the big club.

> This country is finished.

What's the difference? The Heartland meme has Carlin blaming the <u>government</u>; but, Carlin actually blamed the "big wealthy business interests" (such as those who fund the Cato and Heartland institutes). There's more, but that is the difference that most benefits the Heartland Institute, and probably why they originally posted it.

To their credit, the Heartland Institute pulled this meme from their Facebook account and apologized for having posted a clearly inaccurate quote as soon as they were informed that it was not true (the original Carlin lines that are closest to those in the meme are shown in the transcript above in bold print). Unfortunately, it had already been forwarded thousands of times by conservatives who <u>want</u> to hear that liberal icon George Carlin blamed government for these things; and, it continues to be circulated long after Heartland pulled it. Removed or not, it is still doing what it was intended to do: mislead the public through a misquote.

That's one of the nice things about misquotes and misinformation on the internet (nice for those who want to disseminate incorrect information): even if it is retracted, it never seems to go away.

Misdirect   A modern example of misdirection occurred early in the debates over the Patient Protection and Affordable Care Act (often referred to as *Obamacare*). In August of 2009, politicians, media consultants, and opponents of the health care act claimed that it would put government bureaucrats in a position to decide who would get medical care, and who would not — to decide "who was worthy of expensive medical care". It was claimed that the elderly, the physically disabled, and the mentally challenged would not warrant such expense and would be denied. Former Vice-Presidential candidate Sarah Palin coined the expression "death panels" to describe these bureaucrats. CBS News reported on August 8th that Palin had said that:

> My parents or my baby with Down Syndrome will have to stand in front of Obama's "death panel" so his bureaucrats can decide, based on a subjective judgment of their level of productivity in society, whether they are worthy of health care

As we saw with misquotes on the internet, these claims never seem to go away. All of the responsible media found her claims to be totally bogus, and only "fake news" sites like Glenn Beck and Rush Limbaugh were repeating it. Nevertheless, polls showed that about 85% of Americans were familiar with the term, and 30% of those believed it was true. That means that more than 1 in every 4 Americans believed it! This despite the fact that "death panel" was named by PolitiFact® as their *2009 Lie of the Year*, FactCheck® called it one of their *Whoppers*, and the *American Dialect Society* called it the year's most outrageous new term.

The result of this claim was that over 25% of the American public was misdirected to a concern which, in reality, did not exist. Rather than discuss or debate the actual features of the PPACA, the discussion was misdirected to a fictitious issue.

Misrepresent   During the 2004 Presidential campaign, supporters of the re-election of President George W Bush publicized claims by former naval personnel that attacked the heroic military record of his opponent, Senator John Kerry. These attacks became known as the "Swiftboat ads", and the expression "swiftboating" came into common use to describe any nasty, unsupported, scurrilous personal attack on a candidate. The attacks on Senator Kerry came from a group incorporated as the *Swift Boat Veterans for Truth* (SBVT; a 527 tax-exempt organization). After the election, the Federal Election Commission fined SBVT for violating the rules of a 527 incorporation by attacking Kerry rather than focusing on political issues.

The SBVT commercials (there were several swiftboat ads) questioned the legitimacy and accuracy of Kerry's wartime service record, and denounced Kerry's post-war activities in the *Viet Nam Veterans Against the War*. Senator Kerry had been awarded a Bronze Star V (for Valor), a Silver Star, and three Purple Hearts (for wounds suffered in battle). Although nearly all of his ship mates came out in support of Kerry, a conservative watchdog group (*Judicial Watch*) pressed the issue and requested the Navy review the combat medals. A review was conducted by the Navy Inspector General, Vice Admiral Ronald Route, and his report stated:

> Our examination found that existing documentation regarding the Silver Star, Bronze Star and Purple Heart medals indicates

> the awards approval process was properly followed. In parti-
> cular, the senior officers who awarded the medals were pro-
> perly delegated authority to do so. In addition, we found that
> they correctly followed the procedures in place at the time for
> approving these awards. … I have determined that Senator
> Kerry's awards were properly approved and will take no fur-
> ther action in this matter.

SBVT also asked Kerry to release all sorts of privacy-protected data; and, he did – but, not until after the election (in June 2005). When asked why he had not done so during the campaign, Kerry responded with the following.

> The call for me to sign a 180 form came from the same parti-
> san operatives who were lying about my record on a daily
> basis on the Web and in the right-wing media. Even though
> the media was discrediting them, they continued to lie. I felt
> strongly that we shouldn't kowtow to them and their attempts
> to drag their lies out.

This is an excellent example of manipulation by means of misrepresenting the facts. It would appear that SBVT was offended by Kerry's anti-war activities after he was discharged, and decided to attack his personal morality and integrity. They also apparently wanted to redirect attention away from President Bush's minimal military experience by discrediting Kerry's "war hero status."

They did this by misrepresenting the facts surrounding his medals with the result that polls indicated a significant loss of trust in Kerry among the voting public. They used their misrepresentation to manipulate the electorate, and did so quite effectively.

How has manipulation impacted some of the other 21st century elections? There are numerous examples that could be cited, but we will restrict ourselves here to just three (in keeping with citations in prior chapters).

Example #19:

Florida Governor Rick Scott

Richard Lynn "Rick" Scott (b. 1952) was elected Governor of the State of Florida in 2011. Scott was born in Illinois, attended college in Missouri, and got his law degree from Southern Methodist University. He served in the US Navy prior to going into private practice at a Dallas, Texas law firm where he was soon made a partner.

At the age of 34 (1987), Scott co-founded the Columbia Hospital Corporation with two business partners (former Republic Health Corporation executives). Two years later, this merged with the Hospital Corporation of America to become Columbia/HCA, and grew to become the largest for-profit health care company in the United States.

Scott served as CEO (Chief Executive Officer) of Columbia/HCA until a dispute arose with the government over their Medicare billing practices. He resigned amidst the furor in 1997. The corporation finally admitted to 14 felonies, and agreed to pay the government a penalty of more than $600 million, which constituted the largest fraud settlement in US history. Scott was not personally implicated, and never faced personal charges.

Investigators for the IRS, the FBI, and HHS (Health and Human Services) served search warrants on March 19, 1997 at Columbia/HCA in El Paso, Texas, and on dozens of doctors suspected of working with the corporation. Scott signed his final SEC report as the Chief Executive on March 27th (8 days later). Just 4 months later, the Board of Directors paid Scott nearly $10 million in settlement, and "encouraged" Scott to resign as Chairman and CEO. At the time, he still retained more than 10 million shares of Columbia/HCA stock (at that time, worth over $350 million).

The Directors had been forewarned that incentives the corporation offered doctors could be illegal under the anti-kickback law intended to avoid conflicts of interest in Medicare and Medicaid billing. The government investigation was concluded with Columbia/HCA pleading guilty to 14 felonies, and agreeing to settlements reached in 2000 and 2002 that had the corporation pay the US government the biggest fraud settlement in history. They had admitted to systematically overcharging the government by claiming non-reimbursable expenses, illegally contracting with home care agencies, filing false reports on hospital space usage, inflating charges to Medicare by diagnosing patients with problems more serious than they actually had, and giving doctors partial ownership in certain hospitals in the chain in return for referring their patients to Columbia/HCA. Doctors would receive loans that did not need to be repaid, get office space, free rent, free office furniture, and free drugs from hospital pharmacies all in return for referrals.

It was a corporate disaster. With the $600 million settlement, interest payments, $17 million repaid to state Medicaid, and $250 million to resolve outstanding Medicare claims, the total cost to Columbia/HCA came to more than $1.7 billion.

Scott was not a subject of the criminal case against the corporation; however, his lawyer did say that it was because of this criminal case that Scott declined to answer questions in a deposition 75 times in a civil case at about the same time. In other words, Scott pled the 5th Amendment 75 times in the civil case – ostensibly to avoid incriminating himself in the criminal investigation. At one point, he even refused to answer whether or not he was either a current or former employee of Columbia/HCA! When asked in 1997 about an apparent agreement he had made with a Texas doctor, Scott replied "I don't know what your definition or anybody's definition of an 'agreement' is, or an 'offer' is, or 'promise' is." Even when he wasn't pleading the 5th, his responses were inherently confusing and useless.

When Scott first took office as Florida governor in 2011, he faced a $3.6 billion budget gap. He covered a significant portion of this by cutting the K-12 education budget by $1.3 billion (actually, Scott had wanted an even bigger cut, but the legislature balked at more). The following year, Scott's education budget cut $304 million from the state universities (expecting they would raise tuitions by ~15% to cover their shortfall). Scott faced a strong backlash from these two cuts, and later tried to restore much of it. Although the legislature did restore the university money the following year, it still raised havoc with tuitions and left the 11 state universities level funded over a 3 year period despite increasing enrollments.

That same year, the business tax code was revised to cut business taxes by $750 million (2012), and $2.5 billion over the next 3 years. As Democratic ads pointed out in 2014, the education cuts had occurred concurrent with the business tax cuts. They therefore concluded that the education budget had been cut to pay for corporate tax relief.

Scott responded in the 2014 campaign for re-election that K-12 school funding was the highest under his administration that it had ever been, and was much higher than that under his opponent (former governor Charlie Crist). In raw numbers, this was true; but, the state has one of the fastest growing populations in the country, and spending per pupil was actually lower in 2014-2015 than it was in 2007-2008 when Crist was governor.

Scott manipulated the public image of what had occurred by misrepresenting what had happened, and misleading the voters by declaring the education budget to be 'the biggest in Florida history'. It was misleading because it was technically true, but led the public to think something that was not true — that he had not cut school funding (when, in fact, he had – and had wanted to cut it even more).

In addition, much of the electorate simply "forgot" his possibly criminal activities because for them it was "too far in the past". Also, many were almost certainly ignorant of the events: to vote in Florida, you only need to have lived there for the prior 29 days; and yet, in the 2014 governor's election, an estimated 24% of the voters were not yet living in Florida when the whole Columbia/HCA scandal occurred (Scott won by ~1.1%, and had won in 2010 by just ~1.2%).

Example #20:

US Senator Thad Cochran

Having represented the State of Mississippi since 1978, William Thad Cocnran (b. 1937) is a very senior member of the US Senate. A contentious re-election occurred in 2014, when he was challenged in the Republican primary by a Tea Party favorite, State Senator Chris McDaniel. Although Cochran later won re-election by a wide margin in this Republican state, the real drama took place in the party primary.

Running for his 7th term, Cochran was accused by McDaniel of not being a 'true conservative', and ultra-conservative groups and donors quickly lined up in support of McDaniel. It was clear that a close race was in store. The 3rd candidate in the race, realtor Thomas Carey polled fewer than 5,000 votes (1.5%), but that was enough to deny both Cochran and McDaniel the 50% needed to win. The result was a run-off election between Cochran and McDaniel. Cocrhan won with 51%, while voter turnout for the runoff was up by more than 63,000 (a 20% increase). Why did these extra voters turn up for the runoff? And, why did nearly 60% of them vote for Cochran? Manipulation.

McDaniel's campaign had significant funding in the form of so-called *dark money* – funds where the donor is not publicly revealed. *Mother Jones Magazine* attributed the primary source of this dark money to the Koch brothers (who we'll look at later). After the 2014 elections, even CBS commented on the increase in dark money for that election cycle, and the *New York Times* called it the "greatest wave of secret, special-interest money ever raised in a congressional election".

This money was spent (by both campaigns) largely to distort the public perception of the two candidates: *misleading* the public in their understanding of what Cochran had done in his prior 6 terms in the Senate, *misdirecting* attention to regional issues (which were non-issues at the national level, where Senators get involved), *misrepresenting* Cochran as being too friendly to the Democratic administration of Barack Obama, and even *misquoting* Cochran's daughter (University of Southern Mississippi English Professor Kate Cochran) by taking comments she made on Facebook® out of context and using them in a TV ad.

In the 2014 Mississippi election for US Senate, both candidates attempted to manipulate (rather than inform) the public with regard to their opponent. It appears, at least from the results of the final primary runoff, that Thad Cochran was simply better at this than Chris McDaniel was.

Few American leaders in recent years, however, have been better at public manipulation than President George W Bush. President Bush managed to manipulate Congress, the public at large, and specifically the electorate — all of them, it would appear, quite effectively.

Example #21:

Presidnt George W Bush

George Walker Bush (b. 1946) was only the second son of a President to be elected President himself (the first, John Adams & John Quincy Adams, occurred nearly 200 years earlier). Bush is a study in opposites: he was loved by many, but despised by even more. His approval ratings varied more than any other President since the Gallup company began tracking them: hitting a high of 90% immediately after the 9/11 attack in 2001, and a low of 25% late in 2008 (after the economy had crashed near the end of his term). The 90% was the highest ever recorded for any president; and, the 25% was close to the historical low (1 point higher than Richard Nixon the week before he resigned; 3 points higher than Harry Truman in February 1952 as the Korean War was stalemated and going no place, inflation was rapidly rising, there was a scandal in the IRS, and he had implemented very unpopular price controls). Even though his approval was not as low as Truman or Nixon, his <u>dis</u>approval rating went higher than anyone, ever: 69%.

Through all of this, President Bush relentlessly tried to manipulate public opinion as well as that of Congress. Evidently, he was very good at it, for he was re-elected in 2004. There were certainly other factors in that election (such as the "swiftboat" attack ads on Senator Kerry), but Bush's self-directed manipulation was even greater.

John McArthur, the publisher of *Harper's Magazine*, wrote that "effective propaganda relies on half-truths and the conflation of disparate 'facts' (like Saddam's genuine human rights violations)." The British author George Orwell called this process *language slovenliness*. Bush would repeatedly refer to terrorism and Hussein in the same sentence — often, though never directly. linking Iraq with al Qaeda.

Aldous Huxley, in *Brave New World*, spelled out the means that leaders often use to manipulate the public: repeated "catchwords", suppression of opposing opinions, and inciting fear and emotional responses. Bush did all 3 of these in the years between 9/11 and his re-election campaign. He repeatedly used words such as terrorism, attack, and security; his supporters (*e.g.* Rush Limbaugh, Sean Hannity, and Glenn Beck) would verbally attack and demean anyone who dared disagree with Bush; and, he kept telling the American public that the security they once had as a result of having an ocean on each side of them could no longer guarantee American security (ignoring the fact that that security hadn't existed for at least 60 years – at least since the attack on Pearl Harbor in 1941).

Carla Binion, in *Online Journal* (April 25, 2003), pointed out that Bush's "you're either with us or with the terrorists", the "oceans can't protect us", and linking Saddam Hussein with al Qaeda became constantly repeated catch phrases whenever Bush spoke. At the same time, his administration was stoking the fires of emotional fear of imminent terrorist attacks. She pointed out that when a few members of Congress (both in the House and the Senate) challenged Bush on his sources or accuracy, they were effectively shouted down by media people such as Rush Limbaugh, Bill O'Reilly, and Glenn Beck.

But, weren't Bush's fears legitimate? John Kiesling, a State Department employee, was one of 3 career diplomats that resigned from their post in 2003. In his letter of resignation to the Secretary of State, Colin Powell (published by the *New York Times*), he said that there had not been "such systematic distortion of intelligence, such systematic manipulation of American opinion, since the war in Viet Nam. We spread disproportionate terror and confusion in the public mind, arbitrarily linking the unrelated problems of terrorism and Iraq".

It was not just war that had Bush manipulating opinion, however. The *Union of Concerned Scientists* spoke out forcefully on what they saw as the Bush manipulation of public opinion with regard to climate change. They wrote that the Bush administration consistently sought to "undermine the view held by the vast majority of climate scientists that human-caused emissions of carbon dioxide and other heat-trapping gases are making a discernble contribution to global warming".

They complained that despite Bush promising that his administration would evolve policies that were "science-based", he had consistently put forth the exact opposite – challenging and raising doubts about robust, valid scientific conclusions, and demonstrating massive political influence over their position.

Even after the *National Academy of Sciences* issued a report (that was requested by Bush) on the *Intergovernmental Panel on Climate Change* findings, Bush rejected their conclusion (they had strongly supported the IPCC findings). He even went so far as to voice complete disdain for the United Nations support of similar findings. He then created the *Climate Change Research Initiative* under government sponsorship to exclusively study "areas of uncertainty".

While groups such as the *American Geophysical Union* (the largest organization of earth scientists in the world) were stating unequivocally that "human activities are increasingly altering the Earth's climate", the Bush administration continued to maintain that there were too many uncertainties to warrant government action.

Bush, in both the War in Iraq as well as in Global Climate Change, had repeatedly **misquoted** official governmental and scientific findings, had **misrepresented** with respect to each[7], had **misdirected** public concerns and fears from those issues to secondary, non-related issues; and, had deliberately (and effectively) **misled** the American public (and Congress) for the benefit of corporate interests that had funded his election campaign.

President Bush has been generally either loved or hated since his term in office; finding someone who is neutral is rare. So, are these findings fair? Did he really do this? Paul Waldman, writing in *The Week* (a British news magazine which also publishes an American edition) addressed this very question.

He pointed out that during the years that immediately followed 9/11, the Bush administration launched what may have been the most comprehensive, sophisticated, and misleading campaign of government propaganda in American history. He rejected the idea that their supposed "intelligence" was accidentally misunderstood or misinterpreted. He maintained that the onslaught of timed propaganda that "sold" the Iraq war was not a simple lie, but was a deliberate, methodical, relentless campaign where "intelligence" was not used to determine the facts, but was used to create propaganda to sell the war to the American public.

He quoted the then White House Press Secretary, Scott McClellan, who wrote that this campaign "had been finalized with great care [to convince the electorate that war was] inevitable and necessary".

The *Center for Public Integrity* conducted a review in 2008 in which they examined all of the public statements made about Iraq by the Bush administration. They found that there were 935 entire-

---

7 For example, the aluminum tubes Bush claimed Iraq had bought to refine nuclear fuel for weapons were actually standard artillery casings; and, the letter he produced to prove that Iraq was seeking raw uranium from Niger turned out to be a fraudulent forgery.

ly false statements (including 260 made by President Bush himself). What these statements did was to enhance the imaginary threat coming from Saddam Hussein, and to terrify large segments of the American electorate. They did this by raising the spectre of poison gas, mushroom clouds, and WMD (*Weapons of Mass Destruction*). It inculcated widespread fear of the future, even though (in retrospect) Bush knew all along that none of it was true.

The message never changed: if we didn't go to war with Iraq and depose Hussein, he would attack the US homeland with these unspeakably vile weapons. Who knew how many Americans would die next time? Waldman pointed out that sometimes this message came with specific (false) claims, with evil insinuation, or even with speculation about what was to come.

Bush (and his Vice President, Dick Cheney) knowingly lied to the American public to heighten their fear so that support for war with Iraq would come easily. It was an exercise in propaganda of which Joseph Goebbels, Hitler's Reich Minister of Propaganda, would have been proud.

President Bush deliberately lied, misquoted, fabricated, misdirected, and misinterpreted the facts so as to mislead the electorate to support his *a priori* "inevitable and necessary" war. In short, he **manipulated** reality for his political purposes.

Chapter 11
Fear

The people don't want war, but they can always be brought to the bidding of the leaders. This is easy. All you have to do is tell them they are being attacked, and denounce the pacifists for lack of patriotism and for exposing the country to danger. It works the same in every country.
— Hermann Wilhelm Göring
(Nazi Vice-Chancellor of Germany)

There are two basic motivating forces: fear and love.
— John Lennon

Men go to far greater lengths to avoid what they fear than to obtain what they desire.
— Dan Brown (from *The Da Vinci Code*)

Voters do not really vote "fear"; but, they often do vote "out of fear": fear of the unknown; fear of the potential consequences; fear of what they suspect; or, fear of what they have been led to suspect. John Lennon was right (above) when he defined fear as one of the "two basic motivating forces"; and, this is nowhere truer than in an election.

Why do parents want young children to be afraid of strangers that offer them candy to get into their van? The simple answer is what Dan Brown wrote in *The Da Vinci Code*: humans "go to far greater lengths to avoid what they fear than to obtain what they desire." Children naturally desire candy; but, if they can be taught to fear the stranger offering it, it will stand them in good stead.

The problem is that fear is such a powerful motivator that it can be (and has been) mis-used by political leaders to stampede the public in the direction of their preference. Nazi Vice-Chancellor Hermann Göring (1st epigraph above) summarized it very nicely: people "can always be brought to the bidding of the leaders. This is easy." Tell them they are being attacked, and that they are in danger (the fear of suffering harm or injury).

Example #22:

Louisiana Governor Edwin Edwards

Edwin Washington Edwards (b. 1927) was elected to the US House of Representatives from Louisiana's 7th Congressional District in 1964, and was re-elected 3 times to serve until 1972. He stepped down from that role when he was elected Governor of Louisiana in 1972. He was re-elected to a second 4–year term in 1976. Edwards sat out the 1980 election (which went to Republican David Treen), as he was constitutionally barred from a 3rd consecutive term.

Almost as soon as he left office in 1980, however, he began campaigning for the 1983 election. He was confident of victory. No, he was more than confident – he was cocky. When asked what it would take for Treen to defeat him, he said it would only be possible "if I'm caught in bed with either a dead girl or a live boy." Criticizing Treen, he quipped that Treen moved so slowly on things that "it takes him an hour and a half to watch _60 Minutes_". Louisiana rewarded Edwards' confidence: he easily won the election, and returned him to the governorship in 1984.

In 1988, he actually lost the post, losing by a small margin to Buddy Roemer; but, once again, he regained it when he was elected for a fourth term in 1992. Friends and advisors had recommended that he not try to win back the seat, and a local newspaper wrote that he could only win if he were to run against Adolf Hitler. That almost came true: in the crowded primary (12 candidates) on October 19th, Edwards came in first with 34% of the vote; racist, neo-Nazi David Duke (see Example #9, page 45) finished second with 32% of the vote; and, Governor Roemer finished 3rd with just 27% of the vote. Despite having campaigned with the slogan "Anybody but Edwards", Roemer endorsed Edwards in the run-off election rather than see Duke elected. Edwards was seen as fundamentally corrupt, but he did support the minorities in the state. Considering that the alternative was an active neo-Nazi, the electorate clearly saw that it was in their "best interests" to vote for Edwards. He won the runoff with 61% of the vote. Democrat Edwards was even formally endorsed by President George H W Bush, and former governors Treen and Roemer (all Republicans). A popular bumper sticker supporting Edwards actually read "Vote for the Crook".

After years of being considered corrupt, Edwards was formally charged and convicted in 2001 on 17 counts of extortion, money laundering, mail fraud, wire fraud, and racketeering. He served 10 years in Federal prison followed by 2 years on parole. Just a few months after his release from prison, a Louisiana poll showed that 30% of the electorate ranked Edwards as Louisiana's "Best Governor". He was legally barred from seeking the governorship until 15 years after the completion of his sentence; so, in 2014, he ran for the US Congress, instead.

Corrupt as a US Congressman in the 1960s and 1970s, he was re-elected several times; then, he was elected and re-elected Governor; following a mandatory term out of office, he was again elected Governor; and, after narrowly missing re-election, he regained the office in the next term after that. After serving 10 years in prison on multiple convictions involving bribery and corruption, an 87 year old Edwards won the primary in the 6th Louisiana Congressional District with 38% of the vote. However, in the runoff election between the Democrat Edwards and Republican Garret Graves (the second place finisher), Edwards lost. He got 37.6% of the vote to Graves 62.4%.

This last election occurred in an extremely Republican, gerrymandered District, and it would have been remarkable for *any* Demorat to have won; and, even Edwards couldn't pull it off. He did, however, manage to get 83,773 people to vote for him despite his background. In his 4th and final election to the governorship, the people were already aware of most of these same issues with Edwards — but, in that election, he *won* with almost the same percentage that Graves got in the 2014 runoff: 61%.

Why? Knowing what they knew about Edwards and his prior terms in office, why would they have elected him in 1992, but rejected him in 2014? *Fear!*

In 2014, he was running against Garret Graves, a squeaky clean newcomer to electoral politics; and, he was running in a District that had been redrawn by the Republican state legislature in 2010 to make it one of the most Republican-friendly Congressional districts in the entire country. What made this election different was not just the district, but the alternative for the voters. In 1992, the alternative was not a squeaky clean newcomer; it was a well-known racist neo-Nazi who rightfully scared the daylights out of a large segment of the population. David Duke did have his constituency (again, see Example #9), but most of the voters (61.2% – 1,057,031) cast their ballot for Edwards. It is likely that almost anybody could have won that election.

A better known example would be President Richard Nixon. Nixon won election in 1968, and re-election in 1972. In both of those contests, fear became a major factor in the minds of many voters. Nixon's campaign strategists made sure of that.

Example #23:

President Richard M Nixon

Richard Milhous Nixon (1913–1984) was born and raised in California, and was raised in the Quaker faith (*i.e.* the Religious Society of Friends). Nixon was a good student (graduating 3rd in his High School class), and was offered a scholarship to *Harvard*. He declined due to family problems (his brother's health and family financial constraints), and attended the local *Whittier College* instead. After graduation, he was offered a full scholarship to Duke University School of Law. Once again, he graduated 3rd in his class.

After working in Whittier as a lawyer, Nixon moved to Washington, DC at the outset of World War II to work for the government. A few months after he started in Washington, he joined the US Navy. Nixon went to *Officer Candidate School* and was commissioned as an Ensign in 1942; he had risen to Lieutenant Commander by the time that he resigned (New Year, 1946). Later that year, he was elected to the US House of Representatives from California. He was re-elected in 1948, and then elected as their US Senator in 1950.

In 1952, the Republicans nominated General Dwight David Eisenhower for President, and the convention chose Nixon as his Vice Presidential running mate. They won, and Nixon spent the next 8 years as Eisenhower's Vice-President. When Eisenhower stepped down after 2 terms, Nixon ran (1960) to replace him, but lost a very close election to Massachusetts Senator John F Kennedy. Kennedy's margin of victory was only 112,827 votes (out of 68,939,550 votes cast — 0.16%).

Eight years later, in 1968, Nixon again mounted a campaign for President; and, this time, he won. The President, Lyndon Johnson (below, Example #24) decided not to seek re-election, and the Democrats nominated his Vice-President, Hubert Humphrey, as their candidate. A 3rd candidate, Alabama Governor George Wallace also ran, and managed to get onto the ballot in all 50 states (something very rare, and very difficult, for a "third party candidate") — creating the *American Independent Party* as his electoral vehicle.

In the campaign, Governor Wallace was constantly plagued by charges that he was a racist bigot, and this tended to blunt his strong working-class, middle-class message. Democrat Humphrey was beset by the fact that the Viet Nam war was raging, and he was part of the administration that had escalated it to where it was.

Nixon played on both of these issues: portraying Wallace as the racist governor who had tried to block African-American students from attending the University of Alabama in 1956 (with Nixon part of the administration that sent federal troops to Alabama to escort the students to class). This not only hurt Wallace, it blunted the appeal of Humphrey as a liberal civil rights crusader who had helped lead the effort to get the 1964 Civil Rights Act passed.

Nixon also played the war issue against Vice President Humphrey. Prior to the election, President Johnson's negotiators had hoped to gain a truce in Viet Nam. Nixon got the information from Henry Kissinger (who was, at that time, an advisor to chief US negotiator Averell Harriman), and maintained regular contact with Anna Chennault. Anna was the widow of World War II Lieutenant General Claire Chennault (founder of the *Flying Tigers*, who had operated behind Japanese lines in China). Born in Beijing, China (b. 1925), she was primarily a journalist, but was very active in Republican politics all throughout the 1960s and 1970s. On behalf of the Nixon campaign, she advised the South Vietnamese President Nguyễn Văn Thiệu[8] to reject Johnson's overtures to participate in the truce negotiations. She hinted that he would do better if he held off until Nixon was elected.

President Johnson was aware of all of this from illegal wiretaps on both Chennault and the South Vietnamese ambassador to the US (Bui Diem). Bui Diem, Anna Chenault, Nixon, and John Mitchell (Nixon's campaign manager) held a secret meeting in New York (July 12, 1968), where Nixon reportedly promised South Viet Nam a better deal than what the Democrats would do. Later, President Thiệu was advised to

---

8 President Nguyễn Văn Thiệu left South Viet Nam days before the South Vietnamese government fell to the North in 1975. He lived temporarily in Taipei, London, and spent the final decade of his life living in seclusion in Foxborough, Massachusetts.

boycott the Paris Peace talks — talks scheduled by Johnson right before the election, which would probably have given Humphrey a bump in the polls in what was a very tight election. Johnson and Humphrey, aware of all this, did not and could not reveal what they knew because it had all come from illegal wiretaps.

With the Paris Peace talks going nowhere without President Thiệu taking part, Nixon campaigned on the fear that 4 more years of the current administration under Humphrey would result in thousands of more Americans dying in Viet Nam. It worked; he won.

Four years later, when Nixon ran for re-election in 1972, his Democratic opponent was South Dakota Senator George McGovern. Senator McGovern, a history professor with a PhD from Northwestern University, proposed drastically reducing the military budget, supported amnesty for draft evaders, supported abortion rights (which would become codified in the landmark *Roe v. Wade* Supreme Court decision the next year), and had been the first Director of the *Food for Peace* program established by President Kennedy in 1961.

McGovern was portrayed by Nixon as a threat to American defense and American social values, and was attacked as essentially being unpatriotic (despite the fact that McGovern had been awarded the Distinguished Flying Cross for bravery while piloting B-24 Liberator aircraft over Germany during World War II). This campaign of fear was also successful, as McGovern came to be seen as the liberal antithesis of a loyal, patriotic American.

Nixon had effectively branded Vice President Humphrey as a war mongering continuation of the Johnson administration, and had instilled a fear in the American electorate of 4 more years of Americans being killed in Viet Nam at a rate of over 46 a day (American losses in 1968 had been 16,899 — for the entire war, American deaths totaled 58,220)! The *Great Society* was the term used for the Johnson administration; and, shown here is a typical Nixon campaign pin from 1968 showing the direct connection he wanted the American people to see between Humphrey and war.

Nixon won a relatively close election — winning by a little less than 512,000 votes out of 73.2 million votes cast (a margin of 0.7%).

By 1972, the dynamics of the war had changed. American deaths had dropped to about 2 a day, and total deaths for 1972 came to only 759 (just 4½% of what they had been in 1968). As a result, Nixon portrayed himself as the leader who was gradually and gracefully extricating the US from "Johnson's war", and Senator McGovern as the lunatic peace fringe candidate who would sell out America if elected. The total unacceptability of McGovern was pressed by the Nixon campaign in two ways: make the public fear a McGovern administration, and remove Nixon's sometimes toxic reputation from the equation. The following two campaign pins from 1972 illustrate this dual-pronged approach. The first shows the fear of a McGovern victory, while the second illustrates the concept of re-electing Nixon without directly mentioning him by name (although there were numerous versions that included Nixon's name or picture, this was a more popular format).

In both elections, 1968 and 1972, voter fears of the possible consequences of their vote led the American electorate to vote against the source of those fears.

As blatant as Nixon's use of fear was, however, he doesn't hold a candle to his predecessor in the office, President Lyndon Johnson. In fact, Johnson's campaign in 1964 often serves as an example in political science classrooms of how the politics of fear can dominate a presidential election. Johnson had succeeded President Kennedy after he was assassinated the prior year, and his opponent was the outspoken conservative senator from Arizona, Barry Goldwater. By the time that the election took place in November, most of the American electorate was scared to death of Goldwater — fearing he would turn the war in Viet Nam into World War III by making it a nuclear war. That was largely, almost exclusively, the work of the Johnson campaign.

Example #24:

President Lyndon B Johnson

Lyndon Baines Johnson (1908–1973) was born and raised in Texas. He was educated at what is now *Texas State University*, and became a high school teacher. He entered politics in 1937 when he first ran for the US House of Representatives in a special election for the 10th Texas Congressional District. He was re-elected 5 times, and served until he opted to run for the Senate in 1948.

In a very controversial primary, Johnson was declared the winner by 87 votes (out of 988,295 votes cast). There were all sorts of irregularities in the voting, and it was finally settled in court in Johnson's favor by Texas Judge Abe Fortas. Years later, Johnson would repay the favor by making Fortas his first appointment to the Supreme Court. He even created a spot on the Court for him by appointing Jstice Goldberg Ambassador to the United Nations. When Chief Justice Warren retired, Johnson tried to appoint Fortas Chief Justice, but the Senate blocked it.

Johnson competed for the Democratic nomination for president in 1960, but lost on the first ballot to the eventual nominee, John F Kennedy. The next morning, Kennedy offered Johnson the Vice Presidential position on the ballot. According to Bobby Kennedy (his younger brother), Johnson was only offered the slot as a courtesy, and JFK had expected Johnson to decline; but, he accepted. Bobby said that Jack actually wanted Missouri Senator Stuart Symington on the ticket.

In a very close election, the Kennedy-Johnson ticket won the election (defeating the Nixon-Lodge ticket by just 0.1% of the popular vote). On November 22, 1963, President Kennedy was assassinated while on a visit to Dallas, Texas, and Johnson was immediately sworn in as the 36th President of the United States. Just 11 months later, President Johnson stood for re-election (with Minnesota Senator Hubert Humphrey as his running mate) against Republican nominees Barry Goldwater and Bill Miller.

In the election, Johnson pulled out all the stops to make sure that the American public was duly frightened of a Goldwater victory. Senator Goldwater's campaign slogan was "In your heart, you know he's right", and this was prominently displayed on posters, bumper stickers, and campaign buttons (see page 116). The Johnson campaign twisted this with stickers and buttons of their own which read "In your guts, you know he's nuts". Barry Goldwater was an intelligent, reflective, literate man who had flown B-52 bombers and retired from the Air Force as a Major General. He was a successful businessman, and he generally responded to charges that he was "rash and impetuous" (traits the public would not want in a President) by pointing out that there was an old Air Force adage that "there are no old, bold pilots".

On September 7, 1964, Johnson stepped up the fear campaign with a quantum leap into insinuation. His campaign launched what became known as the *Daisy Girl*. This ad was aired only once by the Johnson campaign, and then pulled in response to a public outcry over the ad's theme. This was intended by the Johnson campaign (according to his campaign advisor, Jack Valenti) to show Johnson as compassionate and gallant; and, it cost them nothing as it made no difference — the ad was shown hundeds of times on news shows, talk shows, and political analysis shows over the next two months. The ad was so outrageous that it was repeatedly broadcast without the Johnson campaign ever needing to pay for it.

The ad opened with a little girl (3 years old) in a meadow picking the petals from a daisy while counting each petal. She repeats some numbers, and gets some in the wrong order, which only made her more endearing. After she reached nine, a deep masculine voice-over started counting back down toward zero. At zero, the screen flashed with a bright light, and a loud noise. This morphed into a nuclear explosion, and cut to a scene of a growing mushroom cloud. As the nuclear fireball ascends, a voice-over of President Johnson tells the listener that "these are the stakes: to make a world in which all of God's children can live, or to go into the dark. We must either love each other, or we must die." Finally, another male voice-over implored the listener to "vote for President Johnson on November 3rd. The stakes are too high for you to stay home."

The verbage in the ad borrowed heavily from a W H Auden poem, but the message was painfully clear: a vote for Goldwater was a vote for reckless leadership that could easily result in a global nuclear war. A vote for Johnson was a vote for love and peace, and for no expansion of the war in Viet Nam. Johnson won in a landslide (with 61.05% of the popular vote — the highest percentage in history).

In retrospect, Johnson did exactly what he had tried to get the electorate to fear about Barry Goldwater (with the exception of using nuclear weapons). In the two years leading up to the election (1963 and 1964), there were 338 American deaths in Viet Nam, and troop strength was at 23,300 (all in support, advisory or training roles). By the time of the next election (against Richard Nixon in 1968), troop strength had grown to 536,100 (23 times as many), and American deaths had risen to 28,262 in the two years prior to that election (1967 and 1968; 84 times as many deaths – largely because most of the troops were now engaged in combat).

The *Daisy Ad* (or *Daisy Girl*, as it is often labeled) was an extremely effective ad for Lyndon Johnson. It imbued the American public with an extreme and, most analysts agree, irrational fear of what a "President Goldwater" might do. Their reactive fear gave Johnson an overwhelming landslide victory, and provided him with both an overwhelmingly Democratic Senate (68–32) and House of Representatives (294–140).

Goldwater campaign pin   Johnson anti-Goldwater pin

Opening scene from 1964 *Daisy Girl* commercial
(featuring Monique Ruiz, née Monique Corzilius)

Section III
Consequences

Clearly, the American electorate has made some bad choices over the years; and, in other instances, they may have made the right decision but for what were undoubtedly the wrong reasons. As we look at the consequences of these decisions in the following three chapters, we'll look at another dozen examples of where this was the case — several more outrageous than anything so far presented.

And, we have seen several of the reasons why these poor decisions might have been made:

- Memory Loss — when things that might, or should, have prevented the voters from supporting a candidate occurred years earlier, so that they had essentially "forgotten" these factors;

- Attention Deficit — when the electorate was so focused on something that they effectively paid no attention to matters that probably should have influenced their voting;

- Ignorance — sometimes, the electorate was simply ignorant of the misdeeds of a candidate – they either had not yet been revealed, or they had only been reported on the "back pages";

- Greed — when the voters believed that the election of a particular candidate was in their financial best interests, and to have paid undue attention to mistakes or misdeeds might have prevented them from realizing that windfall;

• Hero Worship	nothing else mattered when the public reputation of the candidate was such that he was revered as a virtual national hero (often as a result of his wartime service to the country);
• Tunnel Vision	when the electorate was so focused on one side of a candidate that they just chose not to worry about anything else — *e.g.* "he's anti-abortion, so who cares if he'll destroy public education?";
• Manipulation	when a candidate misquoted, misrepresented, or misdirected public attention with regard to facts so as to mislead them into a wrong decision; and,
• Fear	when a candidate managed to scare the daylights out of the electorate with regard to their opponent (or some pending situation) so as to get them to 'knee-jerk' react by voting for them

These are the eight possible mechanisms for psychologically influencing the outcome of an election that we have seen (they are not the only ones); but, what are the potential outcomes of such influence?

The obvious answer is "it influences who wins the election"; but, there are also more subtle results that arise from this type of electoral chicanery:

• Simplicity	when the electorate deliberately and knowingly selects the more "simple" or "common" candidate, and chooses to reject their intellectually or educationally superior opponent – leaving the country with an intellectually weaker leader;

- Money

when a particular candidate exhibits a marked ability to influence the voting public, they may attract large sums of money from benefactors who hope to realize their personal political goals by proxy through that candidate — effectively taking away the choice of leader from the electorate at large; and,

- Blame

when the effective influencing of the electorate results in the election of an obviously poor candidate, the media (and, to a lesser degree, the electorate) often tries to assign blame for "how this could have happened" — changing the political discussion from one based on issues to one based on finger pointing.

Chapter 12

Simplicity

When a candidate for public office faces the voters he does not face men of sense; he faces a mob of men whose chief distinguishing mark is the fact that they are quite incapable of weighing ideas, or even of comprehending any save the most elemental — men whose whole thinking is done in terms of emotion, and whose dominant emotion is dread of what they cannot understand. So confronted, the candidate must either bark with the pack or be lost... All the odds are on the man who is, intrinsically, the most devious and mediocre — the man who can most adeptly disperse the notion that his mind is a virtual vacuum. The Presidency tends, year by year, to go to such men. As democracy is perfected, the office represents, more and more closely, the inner soul of the people. We move toward a lofty ideal. On some great and glorious day the plain folks of the land will reach their heart's desire at last, and the White House will be adorned by a downright moron.
— HL Mencken (Baltimore Sun; 26 July 1920)

Perhaps H L Mencken was being more than just a little pessimistic in the above quote; but, it does seem that the electorate often prefers the "common man" to the intellectually gifted when selecting their candidate. It completely aligns with the idea taught to so many children that "anyone can grow up to be President" — the key word there being *anyone*. Interestingly, Mencken wrote this about 3 months before the US elected perhaps the least intelligent President in history (Harding).

There are limits to who can be elected, however; the voters have never elected (contrary to Mencken's fears) a "downright moron" to the office of President. Nonetheless, they do often choose the less intellectually gifted candidate. In most election cycles, there is no easy way to differentiate the intellectual capabilities of the two candidates; but, on occasion, there are. And, in nearly all of those cases where the difference was something that the voters could have seen, they chose the "common man", not the brighter of the two. Although education does not directly translate into intelligence, there is clearly some level of connection between the two. Only two major candidates for President have ever held a PhD, but only one of them (Woodrow Wilson) was elected; the other (George McGovern) lost in one of the greatest landslides in electoral history.

To illustrate this *common man* point, consider just a few of the past presidential elections.

Example #25:

Dwight David Eisenhower   Adlai Ewing Stevenson II

Sample Presidential Elections [1952 & 1956]

In a relatively unusual occurrence in American history, the elections of 1952 and 1956 pitted the same two candidates against each other in two consecutive elections (occurring just 5 times: 1824/28, 1836/40, 1888/92, 1896/1900, 1952/56): Dwight David Eisenhower (R) *vs.* Adlai Ewing Stevenson (D). There were obviously many other factors that entered into the decision process (*e.g.* the Democrats had been in office for the prior 20 years, Eisenhower was the military hero of World War II, *et cetera*); but, one factor that can not be ignored is the public's perception of Adlai Stevenson. The general view of Stevenson, the grandson of a prior Vice-President, was that he was an "egghead" — an elitist, snobbish, intellectual who was "out of touch" with the common man. This was a view promoted by the Republicans.

In fact, the Eisenhower campaign was correct: Stevenson was a very bright man. Having graduated from The Choate School (a highly selective, competitive, boarding school in Connecticut), he then went on to Princeton, where he earned his BA in Literature and History. While at Princeton, he was the managing editor of *The Daily Princetonian* (the award winning student newspaper), and was an active member of the *American Whig – Cliosophic Society* (the political and philosphical debate club founded by President James Madison and Vice-President Aaron Burr, both Princeton students at the time).

After Princeton, Stevenson spent time at Harvard before earning his law degree from Northwestern. Eloquent and known for his calm logic, it was not difficult for the

Eisenhower campaign to brand him an egghead. Once told by a supporter that "all thinking people are for you", Stevenson responded with "that's not enough. I need a majority." He was right: he lost both elections in a landslide.

Lyndon Baines Johnson   Barry Morris Goldwater

Sample Presidential Election [1964]

Barry Goldwater (R) was an eloquent and charismatic politician with well defined, conservative beliefs. He had graduated from Virginia's elite *Staunton Military Academy*, served as a pilot in World War II as a Lieutenant Colonel, retired from the Air Force Reserve as a Major General, was a leader in establishing the US Air Force Academy, and pushed DoD to desegregate the military. He was a well respected author who had penned the classic *Conscience of a Conservative*.

His opponent in the election was the sitting President (as a result of the assassination of President Kennedy a year earlier), Lyndon Baines Johnson. Johnson's campaign relentlessly portrayed Goldwater as a rash, dangerous, impulsive intellectual who would lead the country into war. Johnson, a former school teacher, played the role of the hard working "Joe six-pack" from rural Texas – a "good ol' boy" who was the archetypal common man. Johnson won in a landslide.

Richard Milhous Nixon   Hubert Horatio Humphrey

Sample Presidential Election [1968]

In 1968, the public disapproval of the Viet Nam War ultimately led President Johnson to forego a run for re-election. In his stead, following a bruising primary season, the party nominated Vice-President Hubert Horatio Humphrey (D) for President. The Republicans nominated former Vice-President, and 1960 Republican candidate for President, Richard Milhous Nixon (R).

Nixon was well known to the American public from his 8 years as Eisenhower's Vice-President, and was seen as a flawed, but dedicated, hard-working, common man. Humphrey was the exact opposite.

Humphrey earned his pharmacist license from Capitol College; but, after working in his father's pharmacy, he returned to school and earned his BA from the University of Minnesota, and his MA from Louisiana State University. He was politically active, and was a Professor of Political Science at Macalester College.

Humphrey was a respected liberal in the US Senate, introduced the legislation that created the Peace Corps, and was the principal author of the 1964 Civil Rights Act. The Nixon campaign wanted to portray him as an intellectual elitist, and frequently used his middle name (Horatio) rather than his given name (Hubert) in a mocking tone of voice — as a way of making him appear to be the elitist intellectual they were accusing him of being.

Richard Milhous Nixon   George Stanley McGovern

Sample Presidential Election [1972]

As intellectual as Hubert Humphrey might have been, President Nixon's opponent in 1972 (when he ran for re-election) was even more so – and, he had the credentials to prove it. Senator George McGovern had graduated from Dakota Wesleyan with a BA *magna cum laude*. He was an eloquent speaker who had actively taken part in the debate society, and had won the state's Peace Oratory Contest. After attending Garrett Theological Seminary, and earning his ordination as a Methodist minister, he earned his MA in History from Northwestern. Continuing on, he earned his PhD in History from Northwestern, and then returned to Dakota Wesleyan as a very popular history professor. He and President Woodrow Wilson have been the only major party presidential candidates to date to hold an earned PhD.

McGovern's Methodist ordination and impeccable academic credentials made him the perfect example of someone who his opponents claimed would be unable to relate to the common man. This message resonated with the voting public, and the Watergate Scandal and other errors in judgment by Nixon were not yet public knowledge.

McGovern was soundly defeated in the general election by one of the largest margins in US history. President Nixon was a flawed human being (the electorate did not yet know just how flawed); but, the "common man" could relate to him, while relating to McGovern was much more of a stretch.

Ronald Wilson Reagan   James Earl Carter

Sample Presidential Election [1980]

Again, although there were numerous other issues at play in the 1980 election (*e.g.* high inflation), there is no question that the personalities and public *persona* of the two opponents played a huge role in the election. President James Earl "Jimmy" Carter had attended Georgia Southwestern College, and had graduated in the 93rd percentile (59th out of 820) from the US Naval Academy at Annapolis. After 10 years in the Navy, he retired with the rank of Lieutenant (equivalent to an Army Captain), and having been personally selected for the new nuclear submarine program by Admiral Hyman G Rickover. Carter is the only President to ever release his actual IQ from a standardized test; it was 176. That is higher than either Albert Einstein or Stephen Hawking, and is well into the genius level.

In support of the nuclear program appointment, he took nuclear classes at Union College. Post-presidency, he is perhaps one of the 2 or 3 most successful former Presidents (active in public service and governmental advisory roles — resulting in winning the 2002 Nobel Peace Prize). To date, Carter has authored thirty books — many to high critical acclaim. President Carter is introspective, highly religious, detail oriented, and non-confrontational.

His opponent, Ronald Wilson Reagan (R) was a performer (actor) well known to the American public for his folksy humor and mannerisms, and seemed far more self-assured and comfortable with the people. He was also much closer intellectually to the "common man" than

Carter. To emphasize this connection to "everyman", Reagan was frequently photographed wearing boots rather than dress shoes, and often
donning a cowboy hat.

Elections are not the only time that we see a preference for the
average, common man for the role of President. With more than
forty different people having been elected to the office, there are
clearly a few who were very intelligent; but, there were far more
who are best described as "average". It would be a mistake to
describe any of them as a "downright moron" (with apologies to
HL Mencken), but there have been several who were definitely no
more intelligent (and perhaps less so) than the average man-in-the-
street.

IQ tests are not public knowledge, and most of the Presidents
have never even taken one; but, there are other ways of gauging
the intelligence of an individual. Experts can look at the vocabu-
lary, grammatical construction, and logical organization in the
writings of an individual and find a direct correlation with the intelligence of the person. The problem with this is that many of the
speeches, articles and even books attributed to famous people were
actually "ghost written" for them by someone else.

However, it is still possible to look at the extemporaneous
expressions uttered by the individual to gain an insight into their
native intelligence. George Walker Bush was the 43rd President of
the United States. Often criticized by his opponents as being too
dumb to have been President, his educational and professional
credentials make that extremely unlikely.

Bush was the 46th Governor of Texas (1995 – 2000) prior to
running for the presidency in 2000. He graduated from Yale University in 1968, and then from the Harvard Business School in
1975. Although this is impressive on the face of it, he did attend
both schools as a "legacy student" (child or grandchild of a former
graduate). The idea that this was a major factor in his admission is
supported by the fact that his SAT scores (566 Verbal, 640 Math)
totaled 1206 (released by *The New Yorker*) — 180 points below
the median for his class.

The 2000 election was close and controversial, and Bush became only the 4th President elected while receiving fewer popular

votes than his opponent. His two terms were very active, having been impacted by the September 11ᵗʰ attack on New York only 8 months into his first term. During his presidency, he enacted policies on the economy, health care, education, social security reform, same sex marriage, tax law, immigration, enhanced interrogation techniques, and electronic surveillance. He oversaw broad tax cuts, implemented the Patriot Act, the No Child Left Behind Act, a ban on Partial Birth Abortion, and the AIDS relief program known as PEPFAR. He also implemented prescription drug benefits for seniors under Medicare.

With the war in Iraq and the war in Afghanistan both dragging on, the revelations about the interrogation techniques being used at the Guantanamo Bay detention center (often described as torture), the slow response to the devastation in Louisiana from Hurricane Katrina in 2005, the banking system collapse that kicked off the longest post-World War II recession (often called the "Great Recession"), and several other major challenges, Bush ended his presidency as being simultaneously one of the most popular and unpopular presidents in history. He had received the highest recorded presidential approval ratings ever in the wake of the September 11ᵗʰ attacks, while also getting one of the lowest approval ratings ever during the 2008 financial crisis.

Educationally, Bush went to the public schools of Midland, Texas through the 7ᵗʰ grade. When the family moved to Houston, he went to *The Kincaid School* (a Houston prep school) for two years. He completed high school at *Phillips Academy* boarding school in Andover, Massachusetts. It was there that he played baseball during his senior year, and was also the head cheerleader; he has always refused to release his grades from these schools.

Bush went to Yale from 1964 to 1968, and graduated with a BA in history. While at Yale, he served as president of his fraternity (Delta Kappa Epsilon), played rugby, and continued as a cheerleader. His grade average for his first 3 years was just 77 (about the 20ᵗʰ percentile), and his senior year grades were comparable under a non-numeric grading system. Five years later, he entered Harvard Business School, where he earned an MBA.

So, Bush was definitely not stupid; but, his grades do not seem to indicate an intellectually gifted individual either. His speeches were written for him, and his book of reminiscences is neither academically nor philosophically impressive. So, what little we have to determine just how intelligent he actually was is derived mostly from his extemporaneous comments and observations. And, these are not generally impressive.

It should be noted that these quotes were not "cherry picked" to support the idea that President Bush was an idiot; in fact, he clearly was not. His facility to lie so glibly (see pages 102 and 103) shows a fairly agile mind; and, many of his policies show some reasonably deep thought (assuming that the ideas behind these policies were his). The quotes, however, were not isolated examples; they are actually highly representative of his spontaneous remarks.

Example #26:

President George W Bush Quotations

I'm telling you there's an enemy that would like to attack America, Americans, again. There just is. That's the reality of the world. And I wish him all the very best.   — January 12, 2009

I didn't grow up in the ocean — as a matter of fact — near the ocean — I grew up in the desert. Therefore, it was a pleasant contrast to see the ocean. And I particularly like it when I'm fishing.   — Sept. 26, 2008

I remember meeting a mother of a child who was abducted by the North Koreans right here in the Oval Office.   — June 26, 2008

I'll be long gone before some smart person ever figures out what happened inside this Oval Office.   — May 12, 2008

Our enemies are innovative and resourceful, and so are we. They never stop thinking about new ways to harm our country and our people, and neither do we.   — August 5, 2004

I'm honored to shake the hand of a brave Iraqi citizen who had his hand cut off by Saddam Hussein.   — May 25, 2004

I'm the master of low expectations.   — June 4, 2003

I'm also not very analytical. You know I don't spend a lot of time thinking about myself, about why I do things.   — June 4, 2003

[*speaking about Saddam Hussein*]
I was proud the other day when both Republicans and Democrats stood with me in the Rose Garden to announce their support for a clear statement of purpose: you disarm, or we will.   — October 5, 2002

[*to Brazilian President Fernando Cardoso*]
Do you have blacks, too?   — November 8, 2001

You teach a child to read, and he or her will be able to pass a literacy test.   — February 21, 2001

They want the federal government controlling Social Security like its some kind of federal program.   — November 2, 2000

I think if you know what you believe, it makes it a lot easier to answer questions. I can't answer your question.   — October 4, 2000

These are not the statements of an introspective, intelligent, informed individual. Are they the statements of an ignorant man? Probably not; but, they also do not reflect a brilliant intellect.

Periodically, surveys are conducted to determine the smartest and the dumbest presidents in American history. The problem with these surveys is that they usually solicit the opinion of the public, and the public is not qualified to make that determination. There have been, however, several college and university studies to determine which presidents are which. And, although the lists so compiled differ significantly, nearly all of them come to the same conclusion: the dumbest man ever elected President of the United States was Warren Gamaliel Harding. In his case, the populace did not elect their peer, the common man; they elected someone to whom they could feel superior!

So, what was it that convinced the "experts" that Harding was so dumb? Primarily his naïve acceptance of everything that was going on around him by people he had appointed. His choices show almost unbelievable naïveté ("a clear lack of experience, wisdom, or judgment"), and display a remarkably ignorant leader.

Example #27:

President Warren G Harding

Warren Gamaliel Harding (1865–1923) was the compromise candidate of a deadlocked party convention in 1920. Falling into neither
camp, Harding offered a stable compromise and was elected with the
largest popular vote landslide (60% to 34%) in history.

Once in office, he appointed some brilliant leaders to Cabinet posts
(Andrew Mellon to Treasury, Herbert Hoover at Commerce, Charles
Evans Hughes to State); but, he also rewarded his friends and contribu-
tors with powerful positions. These ill-advised decisions led to repeated violations of both his trust and federal law. Harding naïvely kept
these people on well after any rational, reasonable man would have tak-
en action — demonstrating both poor judgment and lack of understanding. He once told a reporter that "I have no trouble with my enemies,
but my damn friends, they're the ones that keep me walking the floor
nights!"

Appointees leased public oil fields to private parties in return for
bribes ($400,000) and favors. There was also rampant corruption in the
Veterans' Affairs Department. Harding appointed campairn manager
Harry Daugherty Attorney General. Daugherty owned stock (and was
buying more) in an aircraft company that had overcharged the government by $2.3 million on contracts, and was also accused of accepting
bribes from bootleggers. While he was AG, illegal wire taps, rifled
files, and copied correspondence were directed at Senators and Congressmen that opposed Harding or Daugherty. Narcotics were sold at
the Atlanta Penitentiary, and when the warden began an investigation
outside the prison to determine the source of the drugs, Daugherty fired
him and replaced him with a close friend, who shut down the investigation. The Superintendent of Prisons, Heber Votaw, had blocked the
investigation; and, Votaw was Harding's brother-in-law.

A Senate investigation in 1924 revealed that pardons, freedom
from prosecution, and paroles were all available for bribes ($250,000
for freedom from prosecution). The AG even allegedly arranged for
permits for pharmacies to sell medicinal alcohol to bootleggers —
resulting in up to $900,000 of illegal alcohol being sold (and, this was
during Prohibition). Some of this bootleg whiskey was even smuggled

into the White House. When Harding discovered all of this, all he did was to have the alleged criminal's White House clearance revoked. This criminal's body was found with a single bullet to the head *at the apartment of the Attorney General.* It was declared a suicide without an autopsy.

Charles Forbes, the head of the Veterans' Bureau, defrauded the government of $225 million. Harding eventually demanded his resignation, but also allowed him to flee to Europe to escape prosecution. Harding also appointed Albert Lasker, a cash donor and general campaign manager to head the Shipping Board, where he defrauded the government of millions. The Prohibition Commission was thoroughly corrupt with bribes and payments rampant. Corruption was rampant throughout the administration, and Harding, ineffective and indecisive, spent his time in the White House playing poker while his friends plundered the government with impunity.

Warren Harding may not have been the least intelligent president in history, but he did absolutely nothing to dissuade people from coming to that conclusion. Other contenders for the title of "dumbest President" – on the basis of IQ (as determined by these experts) – would include Calvin Coolidge, Andrew Johnson, Ronald Reagan, and George W Bush.

Presidents are not the only politicians who seem to sink to the lowest common denominator. There are numerous cases of Congressmen and Senators that do or say things that baffle anyone with a shred of intelligence.

Example #28:

US Representative Henry Johnson

Representative Henry C "Hank" Johnson, Jr. (b. 1954) has been the Congressman representing Georgia's 4th Congressional District since 2007. Congressman Johnson participated in a hearing on March 25, 2010 regarding the potential stationing of significantly more troops on Guam. In an exchange with Admiral Robert Willard, he actually expressed his very real fear that if too many sailors were stationed on Guam that the volcanic island might capsize and tip over.

Looking for a "downright moron" to represent them, the voters of
Georgia's 4th District have elected Johnson 5 times — three of them
<u>since</u> that hearing.

One of the more interesting people to have recently held political office would have to be former Vice-President Dan Quayle. James Danforth "Dan" Quayle was personally selected by George H. W. Bush to run as his Vice-Presidential running mate in the 1988 election. He had previously served – without distinction – as both a Representative and a Senator from Indiana. Academically, Quayle was apparently quite intelligent, graduating with a JD (*Juris Doctor*). This can be confusing, however, as the US Department of Education and the European Research Council have both made it clear that they do not consider the JD a research degree, and consequently not comparable to a PhD. Nevertheless, it is an academic achievement that makes stupidity highly unlikely. That does not mean, though, that Quayle was "street smart", or that he had a respectable level of "innate intelligence"; and, he did say some really dumb things.

Quayle made numerous gaffes, never published anything of note, proposed no new theories, nor ever had a significant article published in peer reviewed literature. He was reportedly a C student in high school, but got into college courtesy of his billionaire father's connections. He served in the military, but finished as an E-5, since he could not pass the test to become a commissioned officer.

Example #29:

Vice President "Dan" Quayle

James Danforth "Dan" Quayle (b. 1947) was in his second term as
the US Senaror from Indiana (after 2 terms in the House as Representative for Indiana's 4th Congressional District) when Presidential candidate George H W Bush picked him as his Vice Presidential running

mate. They won the 1988 election, and Quayle served as VP for the next 4 years. Although he holds a JD from Indiana University, Quayle often became the butt of late night TV talk shows for his incredible gaffes — gaffes that can not help but make any objective observer wonder at his innate intelligence. No one ever questioned his luck, however: in November 1978, California Congressman Leo Ryan had invited Quayle to accompany him on an investigative visit to the Jonestown settlement founded by Jim Jones in Guyana. Quayle had prior commitments, so was unable to accept; Ryan and much of his entourage were killed on the trip.

As to those gaffes, however:

- on national television, he corrected a young spelling bee contestant's spelling of *potato* (the student had it correct; Quayle didn't);

- he made statements that made it clear he believed Phoenix, Arizona was actually located in California (even though he grew up in Arizona);

- he once said that Chicago was a state;

- he also said that the United States was technically a part of Europe because the US is a member of the United Nations; and,

- he made the statement that there was both drinkable water and breathable oxygen on the planet Mars (evidently, he is the only politician who has gone to Mars to see).

On some great and glorious day the plain folks of the land will reach their heart's desire at last, and the White House will be adorned by a downright moron. — HL Mencken

Henry Mencken would probably both be proud of his clairvoyance, and also likely despondent over that very same fact: that we may actually be much closer to reaching that point where "the White House will be adorned by a downright moron" than most people thought.

Chapter 13
Money

We had to struggle with the old enemies of peace — business and financial monopoly, speculation, reckless banking, class antagonism, sectionalism, war profiteering. They had begun to consider the Government of the United States as a mere appendage to their own affairs. We know now that Government by organized money is just as dangerous as Government by organized mob. — President Franklin Delano Roosevelt

You can't have it all. You can't get huge tax breaks while children in this country go hungry. You can't continue sending our jobs to China while millions are looking for work. You can't hide your profits in the Cayman Islands and other tax havens, while there are massive unmet needs on every corner of this nation. Your greed has got to end. You cannot take advantage of all the benefits of America, if you refuse to accept your responsibilities. — US Senator Bernie Sanders

Money can have a profound impact on the political process, although, to date, it does not appear to have made much of a difference as to which side wins. The *Sunlight Foundation*, a nonpartisan "open government" advocacy group analyzed the results of the 2012 races for the House, and reported that they found "no statistically observable relationship between the outside spending and the likelihood of victory."

Their primary interest in this study was "outside money". This is a phrase used to describe money spent in the political process by sources that are not under the direction of the candidate, and are generally outside the electoral district. Examples would include political party committees such as the Democratic Senatorial Campaign Committee (DSCC) and the National Republican Senatorial Committee (NRSC). Another source of outside money are the Political Action Committees (so-called PACs). These are groups that raise money from donors, pool their contributions, and then spend that money in the political process. Individual donations are limited, and the process is monitored and governed by the Federal

Elections Committee (FEC). Federal laws passed in the 1970s established the FEC and provided the legal framework for these Political Action Committees.

However, the US Supreme Court ruled 5-4 in *Citizens United vs. FEC* (2010) that the First Amerndment barred the government from restricting "independent political expenditures" by non-profit corporations — effectively treating financial expenditures as freedom of speech, and treating corporations as people. So, as long as these non-profits were independent (not under the control or influence of the candidate), their contributions were declared to be unrestricted. This essentially created a whole new animal, the *SuperPAC*.

Consider the results of this ruling. In 2006, just 2 individuals in the United States contributed over $1 million to an outside political group; but, by the 2012 campaign, just 6 years later, that number had jumped to 126. In fact, in the 2012 election, SuperPACs raised and spent $828 million with 68% of that money coming from just 1% of their donors. A major problem in compiling these numbers is that 501(c) corporations (social welfare, trade association, and other specified non-profits) are neither required to disclose their donors nor report to the FEC; and, they have contributed hundreds of millions of dollars beyond what we see from the SuperPACs. In the political field, these funds from unknown, or undisclosed, donors are known as *Dark Money*.

Although SuperPACs are supposed to be independent of a candidate, 104 single-candidate SuperPACs came into existence in the 4 years following the *Citizens United* ruling — technically these are independent of the candidate, but are often run by close friends or relatives of the candidate; and, as a single-candidate SuperPAC, they are totally aligned with the election of a specific candidate — whether that candidate has any direct control over their actions or not. It can also get rather cloudy. For months, former Florida Governor Jeb Bush would not officially declare that he was a candidate for the Republican presidential nomination. Bush had not "officially" declared that he was running, so he believed that the rules governing SuperPACs did not technically apply to him. As a result of this, Bush was personally, actively involved in the establishement and conduct of a SuperPAC called *Right to Rise*. Two campaign financing watchdog agencies (*Democracy 21* and the *Campaign Legal Center*) filed complaints with the FEC. But, when the FEC effectively said it didn't know how to force compliance, they also filed a request for a Justice Department investigation with the US Attorney General, Loretta Lynch. In the meantime, Governor Bush was raising tens of millions of dollars in an unrestricted SuperPAC which will be used to support his candidacy — even though he is not supposed to be involved in the operation of the SuperPAC.

As already stated, the Sunlight Foundation found no observable relationship between outside spending and the likelihood of victory; but, it is reasonable to believe that a candidate who won a hard fought campaign that had received millions of dollars to run ads on TV, on billboards, and in the newspapers would be grateful to the people who provided the money that made those ads possible; and, logic would dictate that any candidate receiving tens of millions of dollars to help in their campaign might even feel some level of obligation to the source of those funds. In other words, the money might not alter the outcome of the election, but it could still corrupt the position and decisions of the candidate once elected.

Consider a few examples of just how much money has flowed in recent political campaigns and in issue-based decisions.

Example #30:

Thom Tillis   Kay Hagan

North Carolina 2014 US Senate Race

The 2014 Senate race in North Carolina pitted incumbent Senator Janet Kay Ruthven Hagan against Thomas Roland "Thom" Tillis, the 4-term State Representative representing North Carolina's 98th District, who was also the Republican Speaker of the House in the North Carolina General Assembly. A third candidate, pizza delivery man Sean Haugh, was the Libertarian candidate.

A record breaking $118 million was spent on this election, with nearly $82 million of that (~70%) coming as *outside money*. North Carolina is a so-called swing state, and it was shaping up to be a very close election. It was ultimately decided by a margin of victory of less than half the vote total for the third party candidate. About 58% of that outside money was spent on behalf of Senator Hagan, who lost the election; but, does freshman Senator Tillis feel any obligation or debt to the individuals and groups that spent $48 million on his behalf? And, how would we know, since the source of about $34 million was *dark money*, where the public has no idea who the donors were?

Results:	Thom Tillis (R)	1,423,259	48.9%	+45,608
	Kay Hagan (D)	1,377,651	47.3%	
	Sean Haugh (L)	109,100	3.8%	

North Carolina was not the only Senate race in 2014 that was considered critical to shifting the party alignment of the Senate from Democratic to Republican. Colorado was another so-called swing state (sometimes called a *purple state*, since it is mid-point between being a *red state* [Republican] and *blue state* [Democrat]). Just as it did in North Carolina (where they spent $42.[13] per vote on advertising), large amounts of money from outside the state started arriving in Colorado to assist the candidacies of the two major party contenders (averaging an even higher $53.[42] per vote).

Example #31:

Mark Udall   Gaylon Kent   Cory Gardner

Colorado 2014 US Senate Race

In this other very expensive Senate race (second in US history only to the North Carolina race in total cost, yet even more expensive per vote), Democratic incumbent Senator Mark Udall was running for his

2nd term in the Senate following 5 terms in the House. His primary opponent was Republican Congressman Cory Gardner. There were also 2 Independents on the ballot (neurosurgeon Steve Shogan, and IT professsional Raúl Acosta), a Libertarian (humorist Gaylon Kent), and Bill Hammons, National Chairman of the 10 year old centrist *Unity Party of America.*

Nearly $103 million was spent on this election, with just under $70 million of it in outside money. About 6% more was spent on behalf of Gardner than on Udall (virtually none on Kent). Colorado was seen as one of the states that would likely decide the Democratic–Republican breakdown in the new Senate, so there was a great deal of interest in this election by a number of the SuperPACs. Another close race, it was decided by much less than either the Libertarian or the 2 independents vote totals. Since Gardner won, will he feel indebted to the unknown (at least to the public) financial backers who gave him more than $35 million?

Results:	Cory Gardner (R)	983,891	48.2%	+39,688
	Mark Udall (D)	944,203	46.3%	
	Gaylon Kent (L)	52,876	2.6%	
	Steve Shogan (I)	29,472	1.4%	
	Raúl Acosta (I)	24,151	1.2%	
	Bill Hammons (U)	6,427	0.3%	

Assuming that the Sunlight Foundation is correct in that there is no discernible difference in the likelihood of victory, does that still mean that these huge sums of money have no impact? Perhaps the impact is more subtle than who wins and who loses; perhaps it is in what the winner does after they get into office.

Will a Congressman or Senator introduce, or sign on as a co-sponsor of, a bill that they know runs counter to the best interests of the groups that gave them tens of millions of dollars to conduct their campaign? Representative John Sarbanes (D-MD), now in his 5th term in Congress, has spent a considerable amount of effort on campaign finance reform. He has said that "maybe it's the amendment that does not get introduced in committee because the Congressman knows that it is not in sync with the desires of his money patrons. … The donation is lingering somewhere in the atmosphere. It's human nature."

At times, however, the impact can be far more obvious, far more blatant. Nick Penniman, Executive Director of Issue One[9], has said that "on any given Wednesday night in Washington, you'll have a member of, say, the finance committee, standing in the board room of a lobbyist's office, surrounded by bank lobbyists. At some point, someone will hand a staffer an envelope with the checks in it, and the congressman will have raised $100,000 in 45 minutes. And they know exactly who was responsible for putting it together, and whose phone calls therefore need to be returned."

Penniman does see a difference in the motivations behind some of these contributions, however. He sees many as what he calls "ideological givers" (*e.g.* Karl Rove or Mike Duncan). These are donors who give money to candidates who support specific ideological issues with which the donor agrees (Wall Street reform, abortion, foreign trade programs, *et cetera*). But, he also sees "transactional givers" — those who expect something specific in return for their generosity. He says that "these are folks who give just as generously to both sides of the aisle", and Congressman Sarbanes argues that these donors win "regardless of which party wins the election."

There are, of course, ideological givers who also stand to benefit as transactional givers. Take, for instance, the Koch brothers (David and Charles). As the owners of Koch Industries, the 2nd largest private corporation in the United States, they are worth an estimated $80 billion; own oil refineries in Alaska, Minnesota, and Texas; control about 4,000 miles of oil pipeline; and, are the primary financial backing for the Tea Party. There can be no doubt that they are ideologically motivated; but, a successful implementation of their ideology would also result in significant financial benefits for them. They are <u>not</u> *transactional givers*, in that they only donate money to candidates who ideologically agree with their positions; but, they <u>are</u> *ideological givers* who stand to gain tremendously if their candidates win.

---

9 IssueOne.org is an activist group fighting to reduce the influence of money in the political arena. It resulted from the merger of *Fund for the Republic* and *Americans for Campaign Reform*.

Example #32:

David Koch   Charles Koch

Koch Brothers & Libertarian Goals

In 1980, the Libertarian candidates for President & Vice-President were Ed Clark & David Koch. They garnered 921,128 votes — the most for any Libertarian ticket until 2012, when Gary Johnson and Jim Gray received 1,275,821 votes (a larger total, but smaller percentage of the votes cast)

David Koch had a significant hand in 1980 as to what went into the official platform of the party that year; and, it illustrates both the ideological and transactional benefits that he desired. That platform called for the elimination of:

- campaign finance laws;
- the Federal Election Commission;
- Medicare;
- Medicaid;
- Social Security;
- the Post Office;
- insurance industry regulation;
- any tax-supported health programs;
- personal income taxes;
- corporate income taxes;
- minimm wage laws;
- public education;
- the EPA (Environmental Protection Agency);
- the DOE (Department of Energy);
- the DOT (Department of Transportation);
- the FDA (Food & Drug Administration:
- all welfare programs;
- the FAA (Federal Aviation Administration);
- child welfare laws;
- OSHA (Occupational Safety and Health Administration);
- Aid to the Poor; and,
- The CPSC (Consumer Product Safety Commission).

In addition, the platform called for:

- elimination of most safety laws (*e.g.* seat belts, helmets, air bags, *et cetera*); and,
- the privatization of public roads and highways.

The introduction of *big money* has also had an impact on specific issues that confront either the public or Congress, where it is used to advertise and lobby for a particular outcome in what might be a contentious issue.

Example #33:

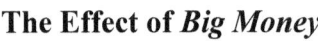 

The Effect of *Big Money*

Although the *Sunlight Foundation* failed to find a "statistically observable relationship between the <u>outside</u> spending and the likelihood of victory", that does not mean that there is no connection between <u>total</u> funding and victory. For example, consider the impact that funding has apparently had in these areas:

- 95% of the 435 Congressional elections in 2012 were won by the person who spent the most money;

- when stricter gun control was a hot button issue, $240,000 was raised to support stricter laws, while $5,600,000 was raised to oppose them (surprise: stricter laws were not implemented);

- tighter guidelines covering the marketing of food to children while in school were proposed and $2,200,000 was raised to support this effort, while $51,000,000 was raised to oppose it (tighter guidelines were not forthcoming);

- the Keystone XL pipeline was an issue throughout 2014 and even into the new Congress in 2015 with people like the Koch brothers standing to benefit significantly from its passage – although $5,000,000 was raised to oppose it (mostly from envi-

ronmental groups, Native American groups, and farm coöpera-
tives), more than $175,000,000 was raised to support it – the
bill authorizing construction was passed by both the Senate
and the House, but was vetoed by President Obama on February 24, 2015 (the Senate failed to over-ride the veto); and,

- CISPA (the Cyber Intelligence Sharing and Protection Act),
  which would allow governmental access to internet data held
  by technology and manufacturing firms for the stated purpose
  of cybersecurity, has proven controversial. Critics argue that
  it tramples on civil liberties and privacy rights; supporters
  argue that it is needed for security. It has repeatedly passed
  the House, but has stalled several years in a row.

  Opponents of the bill are mostly civil liberties organizations
  (such as: *American Civil Liberties Union, Electronic Frontier
  Foundation, Center for Democracy and Technology, Free
  Press, Constitution Project, Fight for the Future, Sunlight
  Foundation, Demand Progress, TechFreedom, Reporters
  Without Borders*, *et cetera*) and on-line petitions signed by
  840,000 individuals. Supporters of the bill include IBM,
  AT&T, US Chamber of Commerce, Intel, Oracle, Symantec,
  Verizon, and Microsoft.

  These civil liberties groups have raised an aggregate
  $4,300,000 to oppose CISPA, while the industry groups have
  chipped in $605,000,000 to support it (a ratio of 140:1). To
  date, it has been repeatedly introduced and passed by the
  House, while failing in the Senate. Even if passed by the
  Senate, President Obama has stated that he will veto it for its
  lack of civil liberties and privacy protection.

Big Money clearly does have an impact, and nearly always falls
on the side where the donors stand to benefit financially from the
outcome. *Outside Money* may not have a direct correlation with
victory, but this may be because outside money frequently flows
into areas and efforts where a pre-existing likelihood of defeat is
already present.

Outside Money is thus trying to alter an outcome. So-called
Big Money, however, is more often tied to competitive areas where
the outcome is not pre-determined. Donors are clearly trying to
affect the eventual outcome; but, they do not necessarily see it as
an "uphill fight". If, in an attempt to influence either Congressional votes or public perception, one side is outspent by the
other by a factor of 23:1 (gun control and school lunches), 35:1

(Keystone XL), or 140:1 (CISPA), it is certainly likely that they will have undue influence (even when they do not eventually succeed). Bottom line: *money talks!* And, *lots of money talks loudly!*

Chapter 14

Blame

The people are responsible for the character of their Congress. If that body be ignorant, reckless, and corrupt, it is because the people tolerate ignorance, recklessness, and corruption. If it be intelligent, brave, and pure, it is because the people demand these high qualities to represent them in the national legislature.   — President James A Garfield

We are taught you must blame your father, your sisters, your brothers, the school, the teachers - but never blame yourself. It's never your fault. But it's always your fault, because if you wanted to change you're the one who has got to change.
                              — Katherine Hepburn (actress)

Let us not seek the Republican answer or the Democratic answer, but the right answer. Let us not seek to fix the blame for the past. Let us accept our own responsibility for the future.
                              — President John F Kennedy

In the final analysis, President Garfied was correct in his statement (first epigraph above). We – the voters – are responsible for the quality of our government and the quality of the leaders we choose. But, that is not necessarily a good thing. It would be if those leaders are all sincere, intelligent, well-meaning, and qualified; but, if they are not, then – as the saying goes – "we get what we deserve".

President Kennedy (second epigraph) had a similar observation, but was more focused on our <u>future</u> decisions — where we must "accept our own responsibility for the future" — *i.e.* don't blame President Bush, and don't blame President Obama; but, as Katherine Hepburn said (third epigraph), we're "the one who has got to change."

Where we so often fail is when, despite having ample knowledge regarding the inappropriate nature of past behaviors, we choose to vote for the same person again (and again, and again, and again, …). But, why do we do this? Albert Einstein once said that "Two things are infinite: the universe and human stupidity; and I'm not sure about the universe." Our voting certainly appears to support that somewhat cynical view, but why do we insist on doing it over and over? Einstein also defined insanity as "doing the same thing over and over again and expecting different results."

- The County Clerk stole from us last time, but he wouldn't do that to us twice, would he?

- The Governor took bribes to make that happen before, but the idea that she would accept another bribe is crazy, isn't it?

- Congressman X spent time in jail the last time he did that, so he must have learned his lesson, right?

Unfortunately, the answers are very often Yes, No, and No.

The fact is that a person who does something once is very likely to do it again; and, prison doesn't usually correct behavior, or so many former prisoners would not end up back in jail[10]. Consider politicians who have done something illegal or immoral; what should we do with them?

- If they took bribes to give special treatment to an accused individual, perhaps we should return them to office.

- If they embezzled funds from the local, state, or federal government, then maybe we should restore them to that office or elect them to another position of financial trust.

- If they display blatant bigotry and racism, and support bills that are oppressive to minorities, why not give them a new opportunity to do this all over again.

The final three examples here introduce three politicians who fall into these categories: one who was convicted of 10 felonies; one who pled guilty to a felony charge after having been arrested and indicted on a 20-count indictment; and, another who actually

---

10 The *Bureau of Justice Statistics* found, by reviewing prison records in 30 states, that 3 out of every 4 prisoners released in 2005 were arrested again within 5 years of release: a recidivism rate of ~75%.

served time in his state legislature while wearing an ankle monitor for a prison-release program (having agreed to a plea agreement to avoid prosecution on 3 felony charges and a misdemeanor).

Who is to "blame" for these felonies, misdemeanors, tax evasion, and other crimes while in office? We, the voters, are! With a federal recidivism rate of 75%, the voters have absolutely no reasonable expectation that things will somehow be different when the guilty politician is *returned* to office.

Example #34:

US Representative James Traficant

James Athony Traficant, Jr. (1941–2014) was a Democratic (later, Independent) politician from northeastern Ohio. He was elected to the US Congress as the Representative for Ohio's 17th Congressional District 9 consecutive terms, having first taken office in 1985.

Prior to Congress, Traficant served as the Sheriff of Mahoning County, Ohio. While in that post, he was indicted and tried on bribery charges. He was acquitted; but, that was not the end of his problems.

In 2002, Traficant was again indicted. This time, the trial jury convicted him of 10 felonies including bribery, tax evasion, filing false tax returns, racketeering, and forcing government paid Congressional aides to work on his Ohio farm. He was sentenced to prison.

After the House Committee of Standards of Official Conduct recommended that he be expelled, Congress voted 420 to 1 to expel him. The only Congressman to vote against expulsion was Gary Condit, a 7 term Democrat from California. At the time, Representative Condit had problems of his own, as his affair with Chandra Levy (a 24-year old intern at the Federal Bureau of Prisons) had become national news. Condit was married; and, Miss Levy had first gone missing, and then had been found murdered and her body buried in Rock Creek Park (Washington, DC). Condit was neither accused nor even named as a suspect; but, suspicion was rampant, and he was defeated in the 2002 primary for his seat in Congress. At the time of the affair, Condit was a

53-year old pro-family politician, and Levy was a 23-year old intern (2 years younger than Condit's daughter, Cadee) originally from Condit's district. Years later, an unrelated male was convicted of the murder, and Condit was exonerated. But, at the time of the Traficant expulsion vote, Condit had nothing to lose: he was suspected by millions of being involved in Chandra Levy's murder; he was branded as a hypocritical "family values" politician who was having a sleazy affair; and, he had already lost his seat in Congress in the recent primary. He very well may have felt some empathy for the vilified James Traficant.

Traficant had always been somewhat of an embarrassment to his party in Congress —despite being well educated (a BS and 2 Master's Degrees), he often dressed inappropriately, spoke out at the wrong times, and was eccentric, flamboyant and confrontational. After the Republicans gained control of Congress in 1995, he voted with them more often than with his own party. He often joked that his wild hair had been trimmed with a weed whacker, although it later became public knowledge that he wore a wig.

Just months into his prison term, he ran as an Independent in the election to fill his now open seat in Congress — *from prison!* He lost to his former aide, Tim Ryan. Less than a year and a half into his prison term at USP Allenwood (the high security federal penitentiary in Allenwood, Pennsylvania), Traficant had to be moved to solitary confinement after having caused a prison riot.

Traficant served 7 years, during which he refused all visitors. While in prison, he received active support from David Duke [see chapter 6] — Duke encouraged readers of his website to donate money to Traficant, and posted a letter from Traficant claiming he had been unfairly attacked by the Department of Justice for attacking administration policies, defying the IRS, and defending John Demjanjuk (the former Nazi collaborator who was ultimately extradited to Germany, where he was convicted of 27,900 charges of accessory to murder). He was released from prison on September 2, 2009, at age 68. Four days later, 1200 supporters greeted him home with a banquet, an Elvis impersonator, and a Traficant look-alike contest. Most of those present wore T-shirts emblazoned with *Welcome home, Jimbo.*

The year after his release (2010), while still on parole, Traficant ran for his old seat again, but was again beaten by Tim Ryan. What was shocking, though, was that despite his criminal past and indiscretions, Traficant polled over 30,000 votes (1 in every 6 votes).

At least Representative Traficant *claimed* that he had been unfairly prosecuted because of his political stance; another Congressman, elected from New York shortly after Traficant was released from prison, actually pled guilty in court. It didn't matter.

Example #35:

US Representative Michael Grimm

Representative Michael Gerard Grimm [b. 1970], a former Marine and former FBI agent, was elected to represent New York's 13th Congressional District (primarily Staten Island and part of Brooklyn) 3 consecutive terms. In April of 2014, near the end of his second term in office, he was indicted on 20 counts of federal tax evasion, fraud, and perjury. Regardless, the good people of New York re-elected him to Congress that November. A month later, he pled guilty to felony tax fraud and, as reported in the *New York Times*, admitted to "committing perjury, hiring illegal immigrants, and committing wire fraud".

In the plea agreement, he admitted to having under-reported nearly a million dollars in income from a restaurant he owned, filing federal taxes based on that incorrect information, and then using the money to pay illegal aliens under the table. Despite representing his District for a Party that is staunchly opposed to anything that facilitates illegal aliens in the US (Republican), he admitted in his court filing to having knowingly employed undocumented aliens who could not legally work in the US. He was asked on December 23, 2014 by a reporter for the *New York Daily News* if he would resign from Congress, and he reportedly responded "Absolutely not!" One week later, on December 30th, he announced his intention to resign.

Earlier in the year, following President Obama's 2014 State of the Union Address, Grimm was asked about the investigation that would eventually lead to the indictment. Grimm at first refused to answer reporter Mike Scotto and walked off; but, the former Marine and FBI Agent then returned, threatened to throw Scotto off the balcony they were on, and told him he would "break him in half." Later, Grimm explained his threats by saying that he "was extremely annoyed".

A special election was held in New York on May 5, 2015 which elected Republican Staten Island District Attorney Daniel Donovan to fill the vacant seat in Congress created by Grimm's resignation.

Although the Consitution is based on the assumption that a person is innocent until proven guilty, we still have to wonder at the reasoning behind New York voters who returned him to Congress in November 2014. He had not yet pled guilty to felony tax fraud, but the threat to the reporter had been recorded on video and played on NY1 (the Time Warner local cable news channel). So, at the very least, they clearly knew that he wasn't someone that anyone would want to "annoy".

It wasn't even close — regardless of the obvious flaws in Grimm's approach to his position, the voters in his District gave him a big pluraility that year, and returned him to Congress by a 53.1% to 40.8% margin over his nearest challenger, Democrat Domenic Recchia. That was a 13,642 vote margin (Grimm polled 58,886 votes). That was even better than he had done in 2012, when he defeated Democrat Mark Murphy 48% to 43%. Not only did his behavior and indictments not hurt his re-election, it appears that it might have actually helped him!

Grimm, however, at least responded to his guilty plea by resigning his seat in Congress. Not all politicians are so motivated. After all, if the "rules" don't require you to step down from your elected position, why would you do so voluntarily? Virginia State Delegate Joseph Morrissey didn't — sort of.

Example #36:

Virginia State Delegate Joseph Morrissey

Joseph Dee Morrissey [b. 1957] is a lawyer, a politician, and a real piece of work! After serving as Commonwealth Attorney for Richmond, Virginia, he was elected to the Virginia House of Delegates (74th District) in November 2007. He was repeatedly re-elected through 2014.

Morrissey had earned his BA in Economics from the University of Virginia, and then a JD (law degree) from Georgetown University. He taught high school government, and then went into private law practice. For two years, he taught law at a college in Ireland, and then at the University of Adelaide in Australia — until they fired him for not having told them that he had been disbarred. The local Australian bar association said that he was "not a fit and proper person to be admitted as a legal practitioner".

While practicing law, Morrissey was cited for contempt of court on ten different occasions, and was jailed or arrested five times. In 2001, Virginia revoked his license to practice law, and the US District Court disbarred him. The US Court of Appeals said that the "evidence ... demonstrates Morrissey's 15 year history of contempt citations, reprimands, fines, suspensions, and even incarceration arising from unprofessional conduct mostly involving an uncontrollable temper, inappropriate responses to stress and dishonesty." Eventually, Virginia reinstated him to the bar, but he remains ineligible to practice law in a federal court.

Morrissey was found in August 2013 by police at his home (in Henrico County, Virginia) with an underage girl (17) who worked for him as a receptionist in his law office. Although Morrissey and the girl both denied any impropriety, a Henrico County court convened a grand jury to investigate whether there was an illegal sexual relationship between the two. On June 30, 2014, Morrissey was indicted on felony charges of having taken "indecent liberties" with a minor, for having possession of and engaging in the distribution of child pornography, and the electronic solicitation of a minor. They also added a charge of contributing to the delinquency of a minor (a misdemeanor).

The prosecutor presented evidence that Morrissey and the girl had engaged in sex on several occasions in his law office in August 2013, had a nude photograph of the girl, and had even sent a copy of the photo to a friend. Even after she stopped working in his office later that month, the prosecutor alleged that Morrissey had continued the relationship, and claimed that they had spent the night together in a hotel room in October. Morrissey denied the charges, and said that he was only trying to help the girl with some family problems (claiming she was being abused by her father). He even alleged that the special prosecutor who had been appointed was "out to get him".

Morrissey refused a plea deal for a single misdemeanor, and then vowed to fight the charges in court. He also refused to consider resigning his Virginia House seat. He made national headlines in July 2014 when he read a text message he claimed had been planted on his phone by hackers — using an obscenity on air.

Later, Morrissey did agree to a plea agreement in which he made an *Alford Plea*[11] to one misdemeanor and received 6 months jail time.

Virginia state law would not have required Morrissey to resign from his seat in the legislature, so Virginia Governor Terry McAuliffe and the leaders of the state Democratic Party called for Morrissey to resign to avoid embarrassment for the House and the party. Morrissey complied, and resigned on December 18th (2014).

A special election was called to fill the now vacant seat, and Morrissey decided to run as an Independent (from jail). Believe it or not, he won the special election as an Independent by defeating both Democratic and Republican opponents in the heavily Democratic district. As a result of the win, Morrissey's jail sentence was later reduced to 3 months of work release.

Morrissey attended the 2015 Legislative Assembly on work release from prison while wearing an ankle monitor. After daytime sessions, he was returned to his cell every evening. A convicted criminal serving time in prison was elected and served because the voters of his district decided he should. The voters have spoken!

As President Garfield said in the first epigraph at the head of this chapter, "The people are responsible for the character of their Congress. If that body be ignorant, reckless, and corrupt, it is because the people tolerate ignorance, recklessness, and corruption."

In other words, we get what we deserve!

---

11 An *Alford Plea* is essentially a guilty plea by someone who insists he is innocent and denies guilt, but admits the prosecution can prove to a jury that he is guilty beyond a reasonable doubt. This was done on the misdemeanor charge so as to avoid probable conviction on the felony charges (which would have resulted in his being listed as a sexual offender).

Chapter 15

The Bottom Line

Democracy is two wolves and a lamb voting on what to have for lunch. Liberty is a well-armed lamb contesting the vote.
— Benjamin Franklin

Experience hath shewn, that even under the best forms of government those entrusted with power have, in time, and by slow operations, perverted it into tyranny.
— President Thomas Jefferson

Sometimes I wonder whether the world is being run by smart people who are putting us on or by imbeciles who really mean it.   — Laurence J Peter (from *The Peter Principle*)

One of the saddest lessons of history is this: If we've been bamboozled long enough, we tend to reject any evidence of the bamboozle. We're no longer interested in finding out the truth. The bamboozle has captured us. It's simply too painful to acknowledge, even to ourselves, that we've been taken. Once you give a charlatan power over you, you almost never get it back.   — Carl Sagan

If voting made any difference they wouldn't let us do it.
— Mark Twain

As has been reviewed in this book, there are a lot of reasons why the electorate occasionally makes a really bad decision. They may not be as colorful as Benjamin Franklin's metaphor of "two wolves and a lamb voting on what to have for lunch", but there clearly are reasons. This is not because democracy does not work; it is not because the voters are criminally involved; it occurs for any one of a wide variety of reasons:

- Memory Loss   the electorate simply forgot what it was that happened that should have changed their vote;

- Attention Deficit   the electorate was so focused on something else that nothing the candidate did mattered to them;

- Ignorance   the voters were ignorant of what had happened, but would probably have voted differently if they had known;

- Greed   the electorate thought that overlooking the misdeeds was in their best financial interests;

- Hero Worship   the voters were so in awe of the candidate that the misdeeds were either rejected or minimalized;

- Tunnel Vision   the electorate was so focused on one issue that all others were just ignored;

- Manipulation   the electorate was deliberately bamboozled by misquotes, misdirection, or misrepresentations designed to mislead them; and,

- Fear   the voters were so fearful of one candidate that they reacted by voting for their opponent.

However, regardless of the reason why the voters ultimately made their horrible decision, there are also contributing factors that enter into these reasons:

- Simplicity   the electorate didn't relate to, or didn't understand, the intelligent candidate, so they voted for the "common man" running against him;

- Money   the candidate raised enough money to inundate the electorate with advertising, media attacks, and

	robo-calls to make the better candidate appear to be the wrong choice; and,
• Blame	the electorate accepted the claims of a bogus candidate that he was framed, that the prosecution had it in for them, or that it was all the result of lies and innuendos.

The result of all this? We occasionally (far more often than perhaps we should) elect idiots, liars and crooks to public office. As evidence of this, consider first an abbreviated (unfortunately, very abbreviated — there have been many more) list of idiots.

Example #37:

Idiots

We begin by defining how we will determine which politicians are, or were, idiots. Technically, *idiot* is a psychological term for someone whose IQ falls within a particular range (historically, someone with a mental age of 3 or less, and in the 19th and early 20th centuries, traditionally someone with an IQ of less than 30). Since politicians are not required to take and submit IQ tests prior to elective office, there is no way of actually determining by this measure if one is an idiot. So, we will use the more modern, colloquial, psycho-historical usage of the term: "someone suffering from a profound intellectual disability".

In the absence of any quantifiable measure for this, we will judge idiocy on the basis of statements or actions that appear to a reasonable human being as being "unbelievably stupid". As Forrest Gump said so eloquently, "stupid is as stupid does."

• **Larry Craig**　　A 5-term Representative and 3-term Senator from Idaho, Craig had a rating of 96 (out of 100) from the American Conservative Union, and had voted against the bill (which passed anyway) that added sexual orientation to the federal hate crimes legislation. In 2007, Craig pled guilty to a misdemeanor disorderly conduct charge arising from an arrest at the Minneapolis-St. Paul International Airport for lewd conduct by soliciting a male undercover police officer for sex in an airport bathroom stall. He did not seek re-election. [photo above]

- **John Edwards** A 1-term Senator from North Carolina, Edwards did not seek re-election as he was the 2004 Vice Presidential candidate on the Democratic ticket with Senator John Kerry. He was an active candidate in the 2008 Democratic presidential primaries (which were eventually won by Barack Obama). He suspended his presidential bid in January 2008, just 3 months after *The National Enquirer* began a series on an alleged extra-marital affair he had with campaign worker Rielle Hunter during which he had fathered a child with her. As the major media outlets picked up the story, he was interviewed by Bob Woodruff on ABC News' *Nightline* (Aug 8, 2008) and asked "a report has been published that the baby of Ms. Hunter is your baby. True?" Edwards denied it, saying "Not true. Published in a supermarket tabloid. That is absolutely not true." However, in January 2010, he issued a press release acknowledging both the affair and the daughter that resulted from it. During all of this, his wife (Elizabeth) had been diagnosed with breast cancer (during the 2008 campaign) and was undergoing chemo and radiation treatment. Estranged from John, she died of the cancer in late 2010.

- **Eliott Spitzer** Eliot Spitzer was a 2-term Attorney General for New York who was then elected governor by the biggest plurality for governor New York has ever seen (two years later, he resigned in the midst of a scandal). A federal investigation revealed that he was paying $1,000 an hour prostitutes, and had spent at least $15,000 on them over a six month period. A published article stated investigators believed the total was about $80,000 over a period of several years — including while he was NY Attorney General (chief law enforcement officer in the state).

- **Mark Sanford** The 2-term governor of South Carolina, Sanford was Chairman of the Republican Governors' Association. During one week in June 2009, nobody seemed to know where he was: not the public, the media, his family, and not even his security detail from the State Law Enforcement Division. He had told his staff that he would be hiking on the Appalachian Trail; but, he never answered any of 15 cell phone calls from his Chief of Staff, and never contacted his family on Father's Day. A reporter found him arriving at the *Hartsfield-Jackson Atlanta International Airport* on a flight from Argentina. He had spent the week with his mistress, Maria Belén Chapur in Buenos Aires. Sanford served out his term as governor, but his marriage to Jenny ended in divorce. In the divorce papers, she said that he liked to "unwind" from the pressures of public office by digging big holes on their plantation with his hydraulic excavator. Ignoring just how stupid this whole affair was, Sanford considered a run for the Republican nomination for President in 2012, and then ran in a special election in 2013 for a seat in Congress which he had held for 3 terms prior to being elected governor. Many of the South Carolina voters might have been idiots as well, as he won!

- **Anthony Weiner** Weiner was elected to the US House of Representatives 7 times before his own idiocy led to his resignation. In May 2011, Weiner sent a link to a sexual photo of himself from his Twitter account to a woman follower. After denying this for several days, he held a press conference where he acknowledged that he had "exchanged messages and photos of an explicit nature with about six women over the last three years." He resigned from Congress; but, he apparently hadn't learned his lesson. Two years later, Weiner entered the New York City mayoral race. It was not long before he was accused of having sent a 22 year old woman sexually explicit photos under the pseudonym of "Carlos Danger". He acknowledged at a press conference that he had, in fact, continued to send these photos, but remained in the mayoral race. The New York City voters were not idiots, and he lost the race with having received less than 5% of the vote.

- **Mel Reynolds** Reynolds ran for Congress from Illinois against incumbent Gus Savage in 1988; he lost. He again challenged Savage in 1990; he lost again. Following the "third time is the charm" approach, he again ran against Savage in 1992; and, this time, he won. During his campaign for re-election in 1994, he was indicted on charges of statutory rape of a 16 year old volunteer in his previous campaign. Despite the charges, he was re-elected; but, in August of 1995, he was convicted on 12 counts of sexual assault. He was sentenced to 5 years in prison (which he served), and resigned from Congress in October. He also served another 6½ years for other crimes (3½ in prison; 3

in a halfway house). When he got out of prison, he was hired by Jesse Jackson's *Rainbow Coalition* to direct their youth program to decrease the number of African-Americans going to jail! In February 2014, Reynolds was arrested in Zimbabwe on visa charges, and was found in possession of self-filmed pornography with several women in his hotel room. He was deported to South Africa. While in Congress, he had actually co-sponsored a bill that recommended life in prison for repeat sexual predators. It evidently escaped Reynolds that, if he were held accountable under the bill that he had sponsored, he would now be serving life in prison!

- **Rick Perry**   James Richard "Rick" Perry is the longest serving Governor in Texas history, but he definitely qualifies for this list as an "idiot". In a famous gaffe during a Republican presidential primary debate in 2012, Perry boldly announced that, if elected president, he would promptly eliminate 3 federal departments. When asked what those departments would be, he couldn't remember! He just stood there looking like a "deer in the headlights". Then, speaking to young Republicans at Saint Anselm College (New Hampshire), he said "those who are going to be over 21 on November 12th, I ask for your support."

     This qualifies as an example for this section for two reasons: (1) the 2012 election was scheduled for Noverber 6th (by law, the first Tuesday in November), not the 12th (which also happened to be a Monday); and, (2) the 26th Amendment to the Constitution moved the voting age from 21 to 18 (becoming law in July 1971 – *when Perry was 21*). Any candidate who spends as much time as Perry does on what the Constitution does and does not allow should probably know what it is that the Constitution actually says.

Perhaps these examples do not indicate a lack of innate intelligence; but, they clearly show a marked lack of intellectual judgment. By contrast, liars may not show a lack of intellectual judgment, but do usually display a lack of moral or ethical standards.

Example #38:

Liars

It is somewhat simpler to determine who is a liar than it was to define an idiot. A lie is defined as saying something that is not true. Now, it is possible to say an untruth when you honestly believe it to be true but do not know the truth; but, that is not the concern here. The *Holy Bible* stating that the earth is flat with edges and rests on 4 pillars is an example of this (Job 38:13, Job 9:6, Revelations 7:1). These statements were not intended as metaphors; but, at the time they were written, the authors were unaware of the nature of both the earth and the solar system.

In this list, we are really only concerned with statements that were a lie because the speaker did know the truth, but deliberately decided to say something contrary to that truth.

- **Ronald Reagan**   Reagan was a 2-term President from 1980 to 1988. During his 2nd term in office, Iran was under an arms embargo; and, at the time, 7 Americans were being held as hostages in Lebanon by a group friendly with Iran. Senior administration officials arranged to have Israel secretly ship arms to Iran, and be paid by the Iranians. In return, Iran agreed to try to get the hostages in Lebanon released. After the sale, the US promised to resupply Israel, and Israel would distribute the Iranian money as directed by the US. The US then had this money sent to fund anti-government rebels in Nicaragua. As news of this ilegal arrangement began to leak out, President Reagan was asked about it. His reply was: "In spite of the wildly speculative and false stories of arms for hostages and alleged ransom payments, we did not, I repeat, did not, trade weapons or anything else for hostages. Nor will we." *We did; he lied.*   [photo above]

- **Barack Obama**   Obama is the 2-term President first elected in 2008. In March 2010, Obama's featured legislative act was passed: the *Patient Protection and Affordable Care Act* (colloquially known as *Obamacare*), an act designed to significantly expand medical coverage in the United States. Opponents of the act (largely conservatives who believed it was government over-reach to get involved in the commercial medical field) made all sorts of claims about what would happen if the act were passed (death panels, higher taxes, bureaucrats making medical decisions, *et cetera*). In response to questions from both the media and the public about people losing their current coverage, Obama said that: "If you like the plan you have, you can keep it." When existing plans failed to offer the minimum required coverages, the insurance companies cancelled those plans, and clients who had these plans had to get new plans (often, more expensive) from the ACA. So, *he lied.*

- **George W Bush**   Bush, the son of the former President, was the 2-term President for the first 8 years of the 21st century. Less than 8 months after inauguration, the terrorist attack on 9/11 occurred. As a result of a number of things, this ultimately led to the US going to war in both Afghanistan and Iraq. Afghanistan was the home base of the terrorists; but, Iraq became involved because it was claimed that they were allied with terrorists and had developed WMD (*Weapons of Mass Destruction* — *i.e.* weapons capable of killing thousands, or even millions, of victims with chemical, biological, or nuclear technology). After US forces defeated Saddam Hussein's army in Iraq, President Bush announced to the world that: "We found the weapons of mass destruction. We found biological laboratories." We hadn't; there weren't any. *He lied.*

- **Dick Cheney**   Cheney was White House Chief of Staff (under President Gerald Ford), a 5-term Congressman from Wyoming, Secretary of Defense (under President George H W Bush), and a 2-term Vice President under President George W Bush. As the administration was 'making its case' for war in Iraq, information gathered by the CIA and military sources was shared with the media. In summarizing this information, Cheney said that: "Simply stated, there is no doubt that Saddam Hussein has weapons of mass destruction. There is no doubt he is amassing them to use against our friends, against our allies, and against us." This "information", however, turned out to be fabricated, and Hussein had no such weapons. In order to get support for the war the administration wanted, *he knowingly and blatantly lied.*

- **Richard Nixon**   Nixon, a 2-term President, is the only US President to ever resign from office. In June 1972 (during his re-election campaign), a small group broke into the Democratic National Committee headquarters at the Watergate office complex in Washington, DC. They had previously installed listening devices on phones in the DNC offices, but these needed to be repaired. The June break-in was an attempt to fix that equipment; but, the group was caught by an alert security guard. As it became increasingly likely that Nixon had known about (and had perhaps even personally approved) the plan, the Nixon administration began an extensive cover-up of their involvement. When questioned by a reporter at a press conference, Nixon said that: "I can say categorically that ... no one in the White House staff, no one in this administration, presently employed, was involved in this very bizarre incident." Time and investigation would prove conclusively that *he lied.*

- **Lyndon Johnson**   Johnson became President after the 1963 Dallas assassination of President Kennedy. In 1964, Johnson was running at the head of the Democratic ticket, and a major issue was US involvement in Viet Nam. At the time, there were just over 20,000 US troops in Viet Nam (mostly sent by Kennedy, and serving as instructors and advisors). The public concern was the possibility of more troops being sent, and being sent into combat roles. During the campaign, Johnson stated unequivocally that: "We are not about to send American boys nine or ten thousand miles away from home to do what Asian boys ought to be doing for themselves." He did. *He lied.*

- **Joseph McCarthy** Joseph McCarthy was a 2-term Senator from Wisconsin first elected after World War II in 1946. He soon became the most visible anti-Communist in the Senate, and was convinced that Communist agents had infiltrated the US federal government. *McCarthyism* soon even became a common euphemism for virulent anti-communism. In 1950, in a speech in Wheeling, West Virginia, McCarthy said that "I have here in my hand a list of 205 ... a list of names that were made known to the Secretary of State as being members of the Communist Party and who nevertheless are still working and shaping policy in the State Department." McCarthy never produced that list, never told anyone who was on it, and never had any substantiating evidence. In other words, there was no list, and *he lied.*

- **Bill Clinton**   William "Bill" Clinton had served as Governor of Arkansas for 12 of the 14 years prior to being elected President in 1992; he served 2 terms. In 1998, he was impeached for *obstruction of justice* and *perjury before a grand jury*. The charges were related to an investigation into a sex scandal involving 22 year-old White House employee Monica Lewinsky [right]. Impeachment is the House equivalent of an indictment; but, the actual trial is conducted by the Senate.  Although impeached, Clinton was not found guilty by the Senate. The House believed he had committed perjury when he said, under oath, "I did not have sexual relations with that woman." The Senate disagreed, but likely on the basis of definition (they had not had conventional vaginal intercourse). In the broader, colloquial definition of sex (including oral sex), they most certainly had, and *he lied*.

Lies are often difficult to assess: they may have simply been a misunderstanding of the statement; they may have been told in an effort to "protect" the listener; or, they may have been told for the more traditional reason — to deceive the listener into believing something that is not true.

Similarly, defining someone as an idiot (even using the colloquial definition) is difficult. Someone may truly be mentally challenged; they may exhibit such a self-centered view of the world that they violate both common sense and any reasonable actions; or, they may exhibit such a blatant lack of moral and ethical norms that both their judgment and innate intelligence are questioned by the electorate.

However, the final category here is *crooks*; and, this is much easier to evaluate, as someone being declared a crook is usually accomplished through a criminal trial in a court of law. The term may be thrown about colloquially by the public, but we won't even consider those cases. We will restrict outselves here to crooks who have earned that designation through the "traditional method" — a legal, criminal judgment.

Example #39:

Crooks

Even though, on the surface of it, *crook* appears to be the easiest of all three of these terms to define (as just stated); that isn't always the case. Crook is defined by most dictionaries as a synonym for criminal. But, in doing so, it does not tell us what the crime was that the person committed. So, for this list, we will use a much stricter, narrower definition of the term.

The synonym that we will use here is "thief". A thief is a criminal who is guilty of stealing another person's property. Since that is illegal, a thief is a criminal; and, by extension, a crook. In this list of crooks, the property that was stolen was property that rightfully belonged to the public at large. In other words, a crook here is a politician who stole from the electorate, the public.

- **William Langer** From 1916 to 1920, William Langer served as the Attorney General of North Dakota (having run on the NPL ticket – the *NonPartisan League*). After a falling out with the party, he was out of office for the next 12 years, but did run for Governor in 1932 on the NPL ticket. He won, and then instituted a policy whereby all state employees were required to donate a portion of their salary to the Party and to a weekly newspaper owned by high ranking members of his administration. Technically, this was not illegal under North Dakota law; but, they ran into a problem. This was during the Great Depression, and highway workers were often paid as part of a federal relief program; the US Atrorney had Langer and 5 others indicted on charges of trying to defraud the federal government. They were found guilty in 1934. Based on this felony conviction, the North Dakota Supreme Court removed Langer from office and installed the Lieutenant Governor in his place. Langer and some friends in his administration initially barricaded themselves in the governor's mansion, seceded from the United States, and declared North Dakota independent – until the justices of the Supreme Court would meet with him.

The convictions were overturned on appeal, and Langer was retried in 1935 (a hung jury), and again later in 1935 (acquitted). He was returned to the Governor's office by the voters in the 1936 election, and was re-elected in 1938 (both by a landslide). In 1940, Langer ran for the Senate and won with 38% of the vote in a 3-way race. The Senate, however, accused him of "moral turpi-tude", and initially refused to seat him. That was even-tually over-ridden by the full Senate, and he took his seat. As a Senator: he wanted the US to stay out of World War II; was one of only 2 Senators to vote against the United Nations charter; and, proposed a bill for the federal gov-ernment to pay the costs to ship all African-Americans back to Africa. Langer was elected to the Senate 4 times, and died in office in November of 1959.

Why is Langer a crook if he was finally acquitted of the charges back in 1935? Because, whether legal or not under North Dakota law, he was forcing state employ-ees to turn over a percentage of their paycheck to his poli-tical party and his friends. When the Senate Committee reviewed his seat, testimony was given that recounted Langer collecting fees for imaginary services, taking kick-backs, accepting $56,000 for approving questionable bonds, and receiving $25,000 to lower the taxes for the Great Northern Railway Company. Call it what you want, he was a thief! [photo above is of William Langer]

- **Rod Blagojevich** Blagojevich served 3 terms as Representative for Illionois' 5th Congressional District before being elect-ed Illinois Governor in 2002. Re-elected in 2006, he was removed from office in January 2009. A federal investiga-tion was launched into his activities, and he was arrested and charged with trying to sell political appointments. The Illinois State House did not wait for the trial, and im-peached him on a 114–1 vote, The Illinois State Senate then found him guilty, removed him from office, and bar-red him from ever holding public office in Illinois again (in two separate votes that both went 59– 0). He was then indicted by a federal grand jury that April, and was even-tually found guilty on a total of 18 counts of corruption and extortion of state funds. He is currently serving a 14 year prison sentence in federal prison.

- **Nick Mavroules** Representative Nicholas Mavroules was elected to 7 terms in Congress after having served 12 years as the Mayor of Peabody, Massachusetts. He was indicted on 17 counts of corruption in a 1992 federal investigation into misuse of his office for personal gain (extortion, illegal gifts, and income tax evasion); he pled guilty to 15 counts the following April and was sentenced to fifteen months in prison.

- **Adam Powell**   Adam Clayton Powell was a long-serving (13 term) Congressman from New York. How did he steal? He used federal funds to pay a healthy salary to his wife for nearly 7 years while she was not even in Washington (she had moved back to Puerto Rico), and he had used Congressional funds to pay for attractive young women to accompany him on foreign trips and to his vacation home in the Bahamas. Congressional funds are derived from tax money; tax money is money paid by the people to pay legitimate government expenses; using it to fraudulently pay his wife and take girls on trips was theft.

- **Tom Lane**   Representative Thomas Lane's political career culminated in 11 consecutive terms in the US House of Representatives, beginning in 1941. Lane was charged with income tax evasion for lying to the IRS in 1949, 1950, and 1951. The prosecutors determined that Lane had evaded $38,542 in income taxes (an IRS way of saying that he stole that amount of money from the honest taxpayers of the United States). Lane never denied it, and never disputed the amount (which probably means that it was more), and pled guilty to the charge of tax fraud.

- **James Curley**   James Michael Curley was elected to the Boston Board of Aldermen in 1904 *while he was in prison* serving time for corruption. Later, in the 1940s, Curley was in his second term in Congress when he was convicted of bribery and corruption. After all, why steal from the people of Boston when you can steal from the entire US population? Curley was, without question, a crook.

- **Rita Crundwell** We have saved the most blatant crook for last. Rita A (Humphrey) Crundwell served as the Comptroller and Treasurer for the city of Dixon, Illinois for nearly 30 years (1983 to 2012). In her private life, she operated one of the most respected American Quarter Horse breeding operations in the country (having produced the winner in 52 world championships). The problem was how she funded this successful equine business: she embezzled over 53 million dollars during her years in office. Is this real? Fifty-three *million* dollars? We can assume this is true, as she pled guilty, and was sentenced to 20 years in federal prison (she is slated for release in 2030).

It really doesn't matter why it is that the electorate chooses to elect the wrong people to office. It could be that they forgot, were not paying attention, got greedy, thought the candidate to be above that level of dishonesty, focused on one aspect of the candidate to the exclusion of all others, got lied to and got confused, or feared and hated an opponent so much that they just didn't care.

They may have voted for someone that was "more like them" than the *egghead* against whom they were running; they may have been inundated with expensive, negative ads until they became jaundiced about the whole election process; or, they dealt with their *cognitive dissonance* by accepting lame claims that the stories just were not true.

It really doesn't matter. What matters is that, regardless of the reasons why the electorate does it, they often manage to elect liars, idiots, and crooks. No government can tolerate this level of corruption indefinitely; and, there are really only two possible outcomes when it continues to occur:

- the electorate can come to the sudden awareness of what they are doing, and take a more balanced, active, and critical role in selecting those candidates that will represent them (and their interests); or,

- the moneyed forces that are corrupting the system will gain complete control over the selection of these representatives while the liars and idiots are baffled and incapable of doing anything about it.

In the first scenario, the United States once again becomes what it once was, and what it was always intended to be: a beacon of light and freedom where the most ambitious, smartest, and hardest working citizens can attain success, wealth, power and influence — without losing the heart to protect, care for, and help those who are less able, less capable, or less fortunate.

In the second scenario, the United States returns to what it has spent centuries leaving behind — a heartless, financially bifurcated, feudal society where 1% own or control everything, and 99% have nothing, or next to nothing, at all.

The United States does not need to become a radically socialist, anti-corporate, pseudo-communist state; but, it does need to ensure that it does not turn into an unrestricted, unfettered, uncontrolled, capitalist bastion where only the few — the very, very, very few — have even a chance of success.

Which scenario we follow is up to the voters; and, the country is getting precariously close to the "tipping point" where it will be too late to change directions if we don't like the way it is going. The voters need to decide what they really want the United States to be, and to then take an active role in determining which candidates are most likely to bring that outcome about; but, that would require commitment and hard work. It can't be done by just sitting at home listening (and worse, believing) what they are told by a media that is largely already controlled by that 1%.

We'll close with a quote attributed to Benjamin Franklin that offers some hope that we can have the scenario we desire. It almost certainly did not originate with Franklin, as many pundits ascribe sayings to the Founding Fathers to give them more weight; but, it is certainly in keeping with the insight and raw intellect of Franklin. The message is clear: you can't be blamed for having been born ignorant; but, you do have to take responsibility for being stupid. Voters — *don't be stupid!*

> *We are all born ignorant,*
> *but one must work hard to remain*
> *stupid.*

— Benjamin Franklin (perhaps)

www.ingramcontent.com/pod-product-compliance
Lightning Source LLC
Chambersburg PA
CBHW070909290526
45795CB00001B/265